T0328679

Cambridge Elements ≡

Elements in Eighteenth-Century Connections
edited by
Eve Tavor Bannet
University of Oklahoma
Markman Ellis
Queen Mary University of London

A PERFORMANCE HISTORY OF *THE FAIR PENITENT*

Elaine M. McGirr
University of Bristol

CAMBRIDGE
UNIVERSITY PRESS

Shaftesbury Road, Cambridge CB2 8EA, United Kingdom

One Liberty Plaza, 20th Floor, New York, NY 10006, USA

477 Williamstown Road, Port Melbourne, VIC 3207, Australia

314–321, 3rd Floor, Plot 3, Splendor Forum, Jasola District Centre,
New Delhi – 110025, India

103 Penang Road, #05–06/07, Visioncrest Commercial, Singapore 238467

Cambridge University Press is part of Cambridge University Press & Assessment, a
department of the University of Cambridge.

We share the University's mission to contribute to society through the pursuit of
education, learning and research at the highest international levels of excellence.

www.cambridge.org
Information on this title: www.cambridge.org/9781009485968

DOI: 10.1017/9781009351850

© Elaine M. McGirr 2024

This publication is in copyright. Subject to statutory exception and to the provisions
of relevant collective licensing agreements, no reproduction of any part may take
place without the written permission of Cambridge University Press & Assessment.

When citing this work, please include a reference to the DOI 10.1017/9781009351850

First published 2024

A catalogue record for this publication is available from the British Library.

ISBN 978-1-009-48596-8 Hardback
ISBN 978-1-009-35184-3 Paperback
ISSN 2632-5578 (online)
ISSN 2632-556X (print)

Cambridge University Press & Assessment has no responsibility for the persistence
or accuracy of URLs for external or third-party internet websites referred to in this
publication and does not guarantee that any content on such websites is, or will
remain, accurate or appropriate.

A Performance History of *The Fair Penitent*

Elements in Eighteenth-Century Connections

DOI: 10.1017/9781009351850
First published online: February 2024

Elaine M. McGirr
University of Bristol

Author for correspondence: Elaine M. McGirr, elaine.mcgirr@bristol.ac.uk

Abstract: Theatre is the most ephemeral of art forms, largely disappearing each time the curtain drops and being made anew each time it rises again. It is a truism that the ephemeral performance text is divorced from the static published play text, but this study of the eighteenth-century performance history of *The Fair Penitent* (Rowe, 1703) demonstrates the interrelation of print and performance and models how readers can recover elements of performance through close attention to text. Traces of performance adhere to the mediascape in playbills and puffs, reviews and accounts. The printed text also preserves traces of performance in notation and illustration. By analysing traces found in performance trends, casting decisions, publication histories and repertory intertexts, this Element recovers how *The Fair Penitent* was interpreted at different points in the century and explains how a play that bombed in its first season could become a repertory staple.

Keywords: Rowe, performance, history, acting, Calista

© Elaine M. McGirr 2024

ISBNs: 9781009485968 (HB), 9781009351843 (PB), 9781009351850 (OC)
ISSNs: 2632-5578 (online), 2632-556X (print)

Contents

1 Introducing *The Fair Penitent*

1.1 False Starts and Apocryphal Anecdotes

The Fair Penitent was one of the top-performing (and oft-performed) plays of the eighteenth-century, with at least three hundred and thirty-eight known professional performances in London alone.[1] It was also one of the most frequently reprinted plays: The *English Short Title Catalogue (ESTC)* identifies eighty-five different editions printed in the eighteenth century. Richard Cumberland, in the 'Critique' prefaced to *The Fair Penitent* in his *British Drama* series, groused that 'the *Fair Penitent* of Rowe is one of the most popular plays in our language. More good performers have supported it, more bad ones have mangled, and more amateurs completely murdered it, than can be numbered up' (Cumberland, 1817: xii). In 1785 he assured readers of *The Observer* that a lengthy examen of *The Fair Penitent* was needed 'as there is no drama more frequently exhibited, or more generally read' (Cumberland, 1786: 263). Somewhat surprisingly, given that it was 'the most popular' of plays, it did not strike an immediate chord with audiences and seemed destined for obscurity rather than canonical status.

The Fair Penitent seemed to have all the ingredients to make an instant hit: Nicholas Rowe was a popular, well-connected actor and skilful playwright. *The Fair Penitent* was his third tragedy, and followed the successful recipe established in *The Ambitious Stepmother* (first performed December 1700) and *Tamerlane* (first performed December 1701). As with both his earlier tragedies, Rowe adapted a well-known play for contemporary tastes. His source text for *The Fair Penitent* was Philip Massinger and Nathan Field's *The Fatal Dowry* (1632). This sprawling Jacobean tragedy follows the misfortunes of Charalois as he ransoms himself to rescue his father's corpse from debtor's prison, is rescued in turn by the beneficent Rochfort, is promised the hand of Rochfort's daughter Beaumelle, only to find her in bed with Novall Junior, the son of the judge who had condemned his father. Charalois kills Novall Junior and Beaumelle, and is killed in turn by one of Novall Junior's followers. Rowe makes several significant changes. He moves the action from France to Italy and renames the characters: Charalois becomes Altamont, Rochfort Sciolto, Novall Junior Lothario and Beaumelle becomes Calista. He employs the neoclassical unities of time and place to focus the tragedy more closely on the day – and night – of Altamont and Calista's wedding. But perhaps Rowe's biggest adaptation is to shift the levers of the tragedy away from Charalois/Altamont's inheritance (the fatal dowry) to Beaumelle/Calista's character (the fair penitent).

---

[1] This total, slightly larger than that in *The London Stage*, was calculated through cross-referencing with extant bills in *The Burney Collection*. It is a very incomplete list, as daily bills for the first quarter of the century are largely lost. See Appendix A for a full list of identified performances.

This shift is indicative of Rowe's adaptation strategy: his tragedy focuses on the tangled web of interpersonal debts, obligations and affections between friends, lovers and families. The focus on affective bonds rather than actions makes Rowe's play more difficult to summarise and exceptionally open to reinterpretation as different actors brought different emotional registers and weightings to their characters. One late-century editor complained that 'This Tragedy has the usual characteristics of ROWE – Suavity – Pomp – a sententious Morality – little action, less passion' (Bell, 1791: viii). Passion, it seems, is in the eye and ear of the beholder. Despite these difficulties, the plot can be loosely summarised thusly: Sciolto, a Genoese nobleman, has adopted the orphaned Altamont and his friend and brother-in-law Horatio, and plans to seal this affective bond through the marriage of his only child Calista to Altamont. Unfortunately, Calista has given her heart and her virginity to Lothario, who is her father's and Altamont's enemy. On the morning of Calista and Altamont's wedding, Horatio discovers a letter detailing Calista's love for Lothario and desire to see him once more. He charges Lothario and Calista with their crimes and reveals Calista's unfaithfulness to Altamont. Lothario attempts to seduce Calista again at their meeting, but is rebuffed and then challenged by Altamont, who kills him in a duel. Altamont is broken-hearted by Calista's betrayal and weeps to his sister Lavinia and Horatio. Calista weeps over Lothario's corpse, is confronted by both Altamont and Sciolto, and kills herself as expiation for her adultery. Sciolto also dies, having been wounded in rioting which broke out when Lothario was killed. The play ends with Horatio moralising on the destruction of civic and domestic peace. Much action, for instance the rioting, happens off stage, but the domestic focus on Sciolto's home and its inhabitants creates room for much passion, as generations of audiences attested.

The Fair Penitent had all the ingredients for success, and yet it did not initially take. There is some mystery as to why. Unfortunately, the date of the premiere, which might provide clues about other events impacting the new play's reception – a scandal involving the theatre or its personnel, an event outside the theatre that distracted potential audiences, a rival production, even exceptionally bad weather or an accident in the theatre – is lost. Betterton's Lincoln's Inn Fields company did not regularly advertise in the newspapers, relying on the great bills, which have not survived. *The London Stage* offers 1 May 1703 as a probable premiere date, but that date is inaccurate, as there is mention of 'Mr Rowe's new Tragedy' in the press in early March 1703: 'Next Monday will be published, A Prologue, sent to Mr. *Row*, to his new PLAY, call'd, *The Fair Penitent*. Design'd to be Spoken by Mr. Betterton; but refused. It's [sic] printed in Quarto, and may be stich'd up with the Play', the publication of which was advertised in the paper's next issue (*Post Boy*, 4–6 March 1703).[2] The play's lack of success is hinted at in the sparseness of the historical record: it was not considered sufficiently interesting to document at the time. Contemporary memoirs like John Downes's *Roscius Anglicanus* (1708) detail the theatrical events he considered the most noteworthy; Downes gives short shrift to *The Fair Penitent*, introducing and dismissing it in a single sentence: 'a very good Play for three *Acts*; but failing in the two last, answer'd not their Expectation' (Downes, 1708: 53). Downes suggests that audiences objected to the play's tragic denouement. The death of Lothario at Altamont's hands at the end of Act IV, which leads to the re-eruption of (off-stage) civil discord and the onstage death of Sciolto and suicide of Calista seems to have depressed, rather than impressed, audiences. While the removal of Calista and Lothario, those threats to civil and domestic peace, may have served poetic justice, the play's first audiences seemed to be neither thrilled by the bloodshed nor improved by Horatio's concluding moralising. Samuel Johnson, despite calling *The Fair Penitent* 'one of the most pleasing tragedies on the stage', agrees that 'the fifth act is not equal to the former; the events of the drama are exhausted, and little remains but to talk of what is past' (Johnson, 1817: vi). Downes does not provide any details about the play's run, but his curt dismissal suggests it was even less successful than Rowe's next play, *The Biter* (1704), Rowe's only attempt at a comedy, which he noted 'Sicken'd and Exprir'd' through overexposure in its six-day run (Downes, 1708: 53). By not even specifying a run (he notes *The Biter*'s six nights, and records that *Ulysses*, Rowe's next tragedy, lived for ten successive nights) we can safely surmise that *The Fair Penitent* managed only three days – just enough to secure Rowe an author's benefit on the third night – before it was swiftly replaced.

While Downes attributes the play's poor reception to audience distaste for the writing of its tragic catastrophe, later theatre historians exonerate the (by-then-canonical) play at the expense of the actors. We first see this in 1749, when William Rufus Chetwood, theatre historian and Drury Lane prompter from about 1715 through 1735, publishes his *General History of the Stage*. In this gossipy history, Chetwood makes little distinction between his own experiences and anecdotes picked up over the course of a long career in London and Dublin. A long footnote – almost a stage aside – on *The Fair Penitent*'s initial reception is an example of the later. He tells a well-crafted tale of an on-stage disaster that turned Rowe's tragedy into farce:

---

[2] 'Advertisements and Notices' *Post-Boy* March 13–16: '*The Fair Penitent*. A Tragedy As it is Acted at the New Theatre in *Little Lincolns-Inn-Fields*. By Her Majesty's Servants. Written by *N. Rowe*, Esq; Printed for *Jacob Tonson*, within *Grays-inn Gate* next *Grays-Inn-Lane*, 1703'.

I shall mention as my last Note, an Accident that fell out at this Play, the first Season it was perform'd in the Year 1699, which I gather'd from that Stage Chronicle, Mr. *John Bowman.*

[. . .] Mr. *Powel* played *Lothario*, and one *Warren* his Dresser claimed a Right of lying for his Master and performing the dead Part of *Lothario*, which he proposed to act to the best Advantage, tho' *Powel* was ignorant of the Matter. The Fifth Act begun, and went on as usual with Applause; but about the Middle of the distressful Scene, *Powel* called aloud for his Man *Warren*, who as loudly replied from the Bier on the Stage, *Here Sir!* *Powel* (as I said before being ignorant of the Part his Man was doing) repeated without Loss of Time, *Come here this Moment! You Son of a Whore, or I'll break all the Bones in your Skin.* *Warren* knew his hasty Temper, therefore without any Reply, jump'd off with all his Sables about him, which unfortunately were tyed fast to the Handles of the Bier, and dragg'd after him. But this was not all; the Laugh and Roar began in the Audience, till it frightened poor *Warren* so much, that with the Bier at his Tail, he threw down *Calista* (Mrs. *Barry*) and overwhelm'd her with the Table, Lamp, Book, Bones, together with all the Lumber of the Charnel House; he tugg'd, till he broke off his Trammels, and made his Escape; and the Play for once, ended with immoderate Fits of Laughter, even the grave Mr. *Betterton*
  Smil'd in the Tumult, and enjoy'd the Storm.

But he would not let the *Fair Penitent* be played any more that Season, till poor *Warren*'s Misconduct was something forgot. (Chetwood, 1749, pp. 256–7)

When John Genest came to write his *Short Account of the English Stage* in 1832, he repeated this anecdote almost verbatim, and affirmed the reliability of his relation by noting that his authority for the story is Chetwood, who had the tale directly from John Bowman, who originated the character Sciolto in 1703 (Genest, 1832: 2:281–2). While technically hearsay, Genest assures readers that he can trace the anecdote back to an eyewitness. But it is worth noting that Bowman and Chetwood could not have met until 1715, when Bowman was about sixty-five, and that the anecdote itself was not written down until 1749. It certainly has the hallmarks of a tale honed through the telling, and should be treated with some scepticism. Chetwood's confident assertion of a 1699 prem-iere (a detail Genest tactfully omits in his history), is definitely wrong, and suggests that this anecdote, if not an outright fabrication, may be a conflation of humorous events from different performances, woven together to make the best story. The failure of any contemporary account is another indication that the story is at least grossly exaggerated, for while the absence of evidence is not evidence of absence, especially in this period of lost bills, missing papers and sketchy accounts, we have enough contemporary reports, from John Downes' 1708 *Roscius Anglicanus* to Colley Cibber's (1740) *Apology* – and the story is so very funny – that some trace before 1749 would be expected. Finally, what little performance data we do have contradicts the story. According to the *London Stage*, *The Fair Penitent* was not mothballed after its initial run. It was performed at least once again that season (*LS*, 1960: 2.1:37). On 8 June 1703 Lincoln's Inn Fields staged a 'shortened' *Fair Penitent* alongside an extended 'Entertainment' of singing and dancing for Mary Prince's benefit. The shortening of the play – which would have condensed the five act main-piece into a three or even two act *petit piece* – may have removed the objectionable last two acts, and therefore avoided the problem of Lothario's corpse and/or audience dislike of the dénouement. Or the whole plot could have been condensed into a shorter run time. Unfortunately, there is no way to recover the nature of or reason for the cuts unless a prompter's copy for this performance is discovered. But the June 1703 performance of *The Fair Penitent*, even in shortened form, tells us that Betterton had not banned the play from the repertoire.

Given the improbability of the story, why is it so persistent? While Chetwood no doubt tells the story to amuse readers with a bit of bawdy humour, I suspect Genest latched on to it for a very different reason. In addition to being an amusing tale of a play gone wrong, Chetwood's anecdote provides a plausible answer to a pressing question for the early nineteenth century theatre historian: why did *The Fair Penitent*, one of the most success-ful plays of the eighteenth century, disappear for over a decade after a decidedly underwhelming premiere? For Genest, it was inconceivable that Rowe's writing could be to blame, so he repeated the anecdote that blamed performance. Genest, focusing on the play's contemporary significance, could not fathom its earlier insignificance.

This Element is an attempt to answer Genest's unasked question, and treat the play's changing significance – both in value and meaning – seriously. Rather than salacious anecdotes, I look at performance trends, casting decisions, publication histories and repertory intertexts to tell the story of *The Fair Penitent*'s eighteenth-century performance history. By so doing, I uncover the play's liveness, the ways its meaning and affective weight changed over the course of its long repertory life. Theatre, that most ephemeral of art forms, remakes itself every night. While there are the occasional stage mishaps and spectacular disasters, the more compelling story is the way a play is constantly reinvented to speak to new audiences: performance makes even the oldest plays new again. This Element argues that *The Fair Penitent*'s meanings were made in and by performance: to understand the play, one must understand its performance history.

***

Catastrophic stage accidents are not necessary to doom a play. *The Fair Penitent*'s poor premiere could have been caused by any number of more prosaic reasons that had little or nothing to do with the qualities of either play or players. Plays have failed due to accidents of programming, against political events or unseasonable weather, or simply because there were too many new plays – or too many favourite old ones – crowding the stage that season for one more play to make its mark. Indeed, given the crowded repertoire and limited performance opportunities, it is more surprising that the play was eventually recovered than that it initially disappeared. Whatever the reason for *The Fair Penitent*'s poor premiere, Nicholas Rowe, in tandem with the crowded repertoire and limited performance opportunities that may have led to its disappearance, were definitely the powers that returned the play to the stage. The year 1703 might have been the beginning and end of *The Fair Penitent* if it were not for the runaway success of a late Rowe play, *Jane Shore*, which ran at Drury Lane in February 1714 for an impressive twelve consecutive nights with at least a further seven performances that season. *Jane Shore*'s success led to the belated publication of a second edition of *The Fair Penitent* in 1714, and may have inspired Lincoln's Inn Fields, which needed to compete with Drury Lane but dared not risk tackling *Jane Shore* directly, to return the all-but-forgotten *Fair Penitent* to the boards in 1715. *The Fair Penitent* had four performances at Lincoln's Inn Fields that season: 18 and 23 August 1715, 3 November 1715 and 7 April 1716. The small bill for the first performance on 18 August 1715 is headed: 'Not Acted these Ten Years / At the Desire of several Ladies of Quality' in an attempt to balance novelty, familiarity and fashion (*Daily Courant*, 18 August 1715). The headline assured readers that the play was recalled by fashionable request, and suggested that it was time to 'reviv[e], a Tragedy call'd The Fair Penitent' (*Daily Courant*, 18 August 1715).

The Fair Penitent was revived, but it was not the same play that had premiered in 1703. Even if no changes were made to the text, the death or retirement of the original actors meant that every part had to be recast. The new performers alongside the new context of *Jane Shore* made it a different play. Cast lists for 1715 are missing, but comparing the company at Lincoln's Inn Fields in 1715 with a cast list printed in 1718 suggests that Sarah Thurmond probably played Calista, Thomas Smith played Altamont, John Leigh played Lothario and John Corey played Sciolto. There is no obvious candidate for Horatio, as James Quin, who took up the part in 1718, was playing across town at Drury Lane in 1715. Again, the play failed to live up to expectations: whether it was the lack of sufficient fanfare for the revival, or perhaps an unfavourable comparison with *Jane Shore*, *The Fair Penitent* was not popular with audiences. Over its four recorded performances, takings for *The Fair Penitent* fell from just under £30 to just over £16 – during a period in which nightly costs are estimated to have been about £33.[3] This begs a new question: given the poor receipts, why was the play repeatedly programmed? One answer might be repertory convenience, but the company at Lincoln's Inn Fields had enough plays in rotation that there was no need to keep mounting an unpopular play. It must have had some advocates, and as audiences were voting with their feet, actor power is the most likely explanation for its regular revivals. Indeed, the play was frequently chosen for benefit nights after its recovery in 1715: for instance at Coignard's Great Room in 1719 to benefit the actor Plesaunce Watson; at Drury Lane in June 1721 for the benefit of John Hodgson; and in March 1724 at the Little Theatre in the Haymarket for the benefit of John Rudd, the box-keeper for the Opera. The play's popularity with actors kept it in the repertory, and its popularity with actors also ultimately transformed it into a commercial success. A star-studded production in 1725 convinced audiences to love the play and feel for its characters. The celebrity actors who managed this change were Barton Booth as Lothario, Robert Wilks as Altamont, William Mills as Horatio and Anne Oldfield as Calista. The year 1725 marks the real beginning of *The Fair Penitent*'s performance history. The success of Booth, Wilks, Mills and Oldfield was the first demonstration of the power of celebrity casting to shape meaning and the reception of a play and its characters, a hint every following generation would take to heart. *The Fair Penitent*'s performance history, then, is also the story of the celebrity actors whose performances created new interpretations of characters, shifted the play's focus to foreground celebrity performances, and built new affective relationships with audiences. *The Fair Penitent* of 1725 was not the same play as *The Fair Penitent* of 1703, or that of the 1760s or 1790s. The play always plays out in the present, and actors and audiences bring their own cultural touchstones, social norms and understandings to the performance. The play resonates anew each time it is performed.

1.2 Ghosts of Plays Past: Actors and Intertexts

In his *Apology*, Colley Cibber tells the story of Samuel Sandford, 'an excellent Actor in disagreeable Characters' (1740: 109). Sandford so regularly played the stage-villain that when he tried to play an innocent man in a play, 'the Spectators would hardly give him credit in so gross an Improbability' (Cibber, 1740: 110):

> A new Play (the Name of it I have forgot) was brought upon the Stage, wherein *Sandford* happen'd to perform the Part of an honest Statesman: the Pit, after they had sate three or four Acts in a quiet Expectation that the well-dissembled

---

[3] With the notable exception of the benefit 'for a gentleman' on 23 August, which brought him £115 9s. All receipts as quoted in *The London Stage* 2:1.

> Honesty of *Sandford* (for such of course they concluded it) would soon be discover'd, or at least, from its Security, involve the Actors in the Play in some suprizing Distress or Confusion, which might raise and animate the Scenes to come; when, at last, finding no such matter, but that the Catastrophe had taken quite another Turn, and that *Sandford* was really an honest Man to the end of the Play, they fairly damn'd it, as if the Author had impos'd upon them the most frontless or incredible Absurdity. (Cibber, 1740: 110–11)

Sandford's performance history coloured his reception in new roles: audiences, knowing Sandford's reputation as a stage villain, expected the characters he played to conform to stage villainy and read new characters by Sandford's past performances: a failure to meet those expectations was a failure of the playwright. Sandford's performance history thus affected, indeed derailed, the reception and performance history of a new play, now 'forgot', because the atypical casting violated audience expectations. This is the phenomenon Marvin Carlson calls theatrical haunting: 'The present experience is always ghosted by previous experiences and associations while these ghosts are simultaneously shifted and modified by the process of recycling and recollection' (Carlson, 2001: 2). The ghosts of an actor's repertory haunt new performances, shaping audience expectation and reception: 'within any theatrical culture audience members typically see many of the same actors in many different productions, and they will inevitably carry some memory of those actors from production to production' (Carlson, 2001: 53). While the eighteenth-century British stage was not as strictly codified as that of the French, the limited number of stages (especially after the 1737 Licensing Act) and repertory created a similarly close relationship between actors, roles and audience expectations.[4] The rise of theatrical celebrity in the eighteenth century compounded this – roles are haunted not just by types, such as Sandford's line in stage-villains, but also by the celebrity persona of the performer, which shapes audience's expectations even more firmly than does a performer's acting line. The long repertory life of plays like *The Fair Penitent* adds another layer as memories of past performers, of contemporary rivals, and of the ghosts of those performers' other roles all haunt every new performance. This accretion of ghosts subtly, and sometimes radically, reorients and revises the play itself.

This Element explores several forms of theatrical ghosting. As the overview above of the play's first quarter-century demonstrates, *The Fair Penitent*'s performance history is haunted by the established lines of its actors, whose previous roles establish audiences' horizon of expectations for new characters,

---

[4] As Carlson says: 'this universal tendency was reinforced in a theatrical culture, in which many plays were mounted in a very short period of time, and neither actors nor dramatists had either the time or the incentive to strike out in significantly new directions' (56).

and the celebrity personae of the celebrated actors whose onstage roles reflect their biographies, and who use their performances to nuance or enhance their reputations. It is also haunted by specific echoes of plays programmed around it. Rather than explore the intertextual echoes, the recycling, in *The Fair Penitent* that the playwright may have consciously or unconsciously introduced, I focus on the new echoes or ghosts created by putting plays into repertory dialogue, using the actors' bodies to create a new bridge between the texts. Actors brought the ghosts of their most famous roles on stage with them in whatever part they played, and these echoes were often magnified through conscious programming decisions: audiences who watched a performer in one role would consciously and subconsciously compare that performance to the performance of the same actor in a different role the next night. The limited repertoire gave audiences significant opportunities to compare performers in the same roles, both over the course of several seasons, and in rival productions in the two theatres royal. The repertory theatre of the eighteenth century, in which stable companies played a large number of roles in quick succession, contributed to this phenomenon: actors were shaped by their performance lines, which in turn shaped the parts they played: for a stage-villain like Samuel Sandford, every part he played was a stage-villain. In this way we see how casting had the power to rewrite *The Fair Penitent*: to make Calista more or less penitent; to make Lothario a tyrant or a star-crossed lover; to make Altamont sexy or snivelling; and to make Horatio a hero or a troublesome puppy. Likewise, new intertexts opened up new interpretations. *The Fair Penitent* may have been written as an adaptation of *The Fatal Dowry*, but audiences did not have the opportunity to compare the two plays, for *The Fatal Dowry* was never performed in the eighteenth century. Instead, audiences were encouraged to discover echoes and similarities with plays ranging from *Richard III* (1699) and *The London Merchant* (1732), to *Romeo and Juliet* (1744) and *The Constant Couple* (1699). The diversity of these texts stretched – sometimes to breaking – *The Fair Penitent*'s ability to meet audience expectations and to remake its significance over the course of the eighteenth century.

1.3 The Text and the Performance

The relationship between the performance and publication of a play is complex and multidirectional. Plays printed 'as acted' served as fetishes for performance, allowing former audience members to relive and remember their theatrical experience. Printed plays also served as substitutes for performance, allowing those who had not attended the theatre to engage with it; and as preparations for

performance, allowing theatre-goers to study a part they were about to see.[5]
New editions frequently followed successful new stage revivals, for instance in
1718, 1742, 1768 and 1776. Plays were bought to be used: readers annotated
their copies with memories of performances attended, extra-illustrated them
with additional images of actors and scenes, and annotated them with notes
from other print sources and their own experiences. Within the published play-
text, para texts such as printed cast lists and frontispieces, which act as a kind of
theatrical abstract, defined (and often moved) the dramatic fulcrum on which the
play hinges. Unlike audiences, who (at least in the first instance) could only
respond to events as they unfolded, readers were supplied with an arsenal of
interpretive clues and nudges before they read the play's first line. As the
century progressed, more of these nudges were printed with the play, as editorial
Critiques or Remarks were added to the dramatis personae, and the frontispieces
took on the recognisable features of celebrity actors in role. Late-century
frontispieces and actor portraits not only identify the play's pivotal scene for
the reader, but also reify interpretive choices by presenting a specific actor's
performance as definitive. This reification helps explain the number and variety
of printed editions of popular plays; intertwined as they were with performance,
shifts in performance were met with new editions that published those shifts to
new audiences. This Element argues that just as these many editions helped
contemporary readers and audiences engage with contemporary performance,
so too can they help theatre and literary historians trace how those performance
and interpretive practices changed over time. By bringing the always-present
dialogue between print and performance back into focus, this Element models
ways of reading past performances that highlights both the openness and the
limitations of the reader's or the actor's interpretive freedoms.

***

The printed play can also become a repository for a play's history, and for how
a play intertwines with the history of the book's owners. One such repository is
held in the British Library. This 1763 edition of *The Fair Penitent* (BL11772
a.5) is a pocket-sized (duodecimo) reprint of the original 1703 Tonson edition of
the play. This particular copy is extra-illustrated with newspaper clippings,
including an undated anecdote about the delay of one performance of *The
Fair Penitent* due to the 'domestic misfortune' of the actor playing
Altamont – a case of life imitating art – and a print depicting Genoa, the

---

[5] See, for example the diarist Sylas Neville, who frequently studied a part before attending the
theatre: on 3 June 1767: 'Instead of going to dinner, put "The Suspicious Husband" in my pocket
and read Ranger's part at the Somerset coffee house' (Nevillle, 1950: 9); and 29 March 1769:
'went to see Mrs. Yates do Medea, in which she is inimitably great . . . Read her part before the
play began' (66).

scene of the play. The whole is also annotated in several hands, showing generations of engagement with the text. On the reverse of the title page, one reader has jotted down thoughts about four celebrated mid-century actors: James Quin, who 'performed Horatio for the last time May 1751 as an engaged actor, tho he performed Falstaf for Ryans benefit 1752–1753'; David Garrick, who 'in 1746 performed Lothario in a black velvet suit with broad gold flowers'; Susannah Cibber 'the best Calista' and Spranger Barry, who the reader felt was 'not happy in Lothario'. The *dramatis persona* has also been annotated in this hand with Quin's and Garrick's names added next to Horatio and Lothario. The 1763 publication date of this particular edition accords with these mid-century performance notes, but the reader is paraphrasing – and notes the debt to – Tate Wilkinson's (1790) *Memoirs* in their details about Quin's retirement and Garrick's costume.[6] Perhaps the reader, like Wilkinson, is recalling past scenes, or they might be an amateur theatre historian using Wilkinson to document the interrelation of celebrity and drama. But this keen theatrical reader was not the little book's only annotator: a different hand uses the title-page to note the tragic end to an amateur performance in 1774: 'performed at Step: Foxes Winterslow, Wells Jan[ry] 8 1774 / The seat burnt down / next morning' (Rowe, 1763: n.p.). Yet another reader covers the space around the Act I headpiece to describe Quin's old-fashioned costume: 'Quin presented himself on the rising of the curtain in a green velvet coat embroidered down the seams an enormous full bottomed wig rolled up stockings high heeled square-toed shoes' (Rowe, 1763: 3). Performance notes are dotted throughout: Calista's first entrance, at the top of Act II, is noted with a comment on Susannah Cibber's 'high pitched but jewel withal' voice, while a biting speech in Calista's first scene – 'To be a Tale for Fools! Scorn'd by the Women, / And pity'd by the Men! Oh insupportable!' (II.i.38–39) – is bracketed with the note 'M[rs] Syddons (well)' (Rowe, 1763: 23, 24). The different hands for these comments, as well as the half-century separating Cibber from Siddons, suggest not just different readers, but different readers imagining or conjuring up the accent of different actors to shape their reading and their interpretation of the text: Cibber's 'jewel' tones resonated differently, even in the imagination, than did Siddon's famous voice.[7] These readers were using memories or records of past performances to

---

[6] 'Mr. Whitfield the wardrobe-keeper, produced a very short old suit of clothes, with a black velvet ground, and broad gold flowers, as dingy as the twenty four letters on a piece of gilded gingerbread – this apparel had not been brought to light since the first year Garrick played Lothario, at that theatre in 1746; when Quin acted Horatio, which was the last character that he performed, in the last week for May 1751, as an engaged actor, though he played twice after that his favourite character of Falstaff, for his friend Ryan's benefits 1752 and 1753' (Wilkinson, 1790: 1.115).

[7] See Pascoe (2013).

shape their present reading; this book does the same. The readers of 11772a.5 do not note theatrical intertexts, but they were reading with attention to echoes of other stories and characters. Various readers note a range of allusions from Henry Fielding's *Tom Jones,* noted by two different hands, to Xeno and Dido. The annotations and extra-illustrations in this little pocket edition of *The Fair Penitent* perform the same allusive and comparative work that audiences undertook in the theatre: is a trace not just of reading practices, but of theatrical engagement.

1.4 About This Element

This Element is a response to calls to 'attend to the "deep play" in the stock plays' by telling the story of *The Fair Penitent*'s eighteenth-century fortunes (Roach, 1996: 153). This is not, however, an exhaustive performance history of *The Fair Penitent*, or even of its eighteenth-century repertory life. Many performances are lost to history: the dearth of information about the premiere and incomplete records throughout the century mean that it is not even a complete account of the play's performance history in London's theatres royal. At the same time, the play was so universally popular that it would be impossible for a short volume to offer detailed analyses of all the performances for which we do have records. The play was performed throughout and beyond the British isles: I touch upon performances in Dublin, Edinburgh and Philadelphia, but it was performed in every city with a theatre, and in many places without one. The play was a staple of touring companies like Tate Wilkinson's and West Digges's. It was a favourite with amateur and country house performers, like those at the ill-fated theatrical party at Winterslow House in 1774. Thus, this Element is *a* performance history – other histories remain to be told. I focus on professional London performances for two reasons. First, because these performances left behind enough traces to piece together probable interpretive lines, and second, because these performances were the ones reified in print and 'seen' by readers in the eighteenth century and today.

This Element's aims are somewhat modest: by attending to that 'deep play', it seeks to challenge a model of theatre and literary history that privileges the moment (and author) of writing over that of performance. I move through the hundred years of *The Fair Penitent*'s reign quickly, applying different lenses to performances at the beginning and end of the century. I begin by centring performers and their repertory intertexts, analysing the impact of celebrity on the perceived importance of a role, and the ways in which actors used their performances to inform both their celebrity personae and the characters they played: Section 2 traces *The Fair Penitent*'s shifting affective axis as first

Altamont, then Lothario and finally Calista take centre stage and claim the audience's attention and interest, if not sympathy. Section 3 covers the second half of the century and focuses on the interrelation of print and performance, demonstrated by the proliferation of frontispieces depicting different contemporary actresses as Calista: each actor's portrait promised readers 'the Calista Mr Rowe drew', but each is unique and offers not just a different characterisation, but a different moment of tragic enlightenment. Finally, Section 4 looks at a pair of performances that challenged their audiences' horizon of expectations and make visible the limits of an actor's ability to use their performance histories and intertextual echoes to revise a play's significance. The failure of the century's two female Lotharios is a testament to the power of gender and, perhaps even more significantly, genre conventions in shaping audience expectations, even beyond the influence of a celebrity performance.

The performance history of *The Fair Penitent* is told through its advertisements and reviews, through cast lists and prompter's books, through repertory calendars and through the century of new print editions of the play. Rather than see a conflict in the myriad readings of *The Fair Penitent* by critics, actors and audiences then and now, this Element demonstrates that the play meant differently at different moments: even the question of which character is the lead has different answers in different decades of the play's popularity. Different editions of the play 'as acted' shed some light on these differences. Although the scope of this Element means that I have not offered extensive analysis of all of the different cuts made to Rowe's text over the century, this would be another fruitful approach to demonstrating both shifting performance practices – such as the removal of the song sung to Calista at the start of Act V in the second half of the century – and the shifting balance of stage time and audience sympathies – seen for instance in Altamont's plaintive soliloquy at the start of Act IV which disappears whenever Lothario and Calista's doomed love takes centre stage. Dramaturgy is important. Rowe's text is not static; new editions of the play justify their existence by boasting that their text is 'regulated from the prompt books by permission of the managers': in other words that they offer an accurate account of contemporary performance (Cumberland, 1817: n.p.). While most of these editions of *The Fair Penitent* indicate the lines cut in performance with typographic marks such as quotation marks, other elements, such as the Song, disappear without a trace, only to resurface again later. The text's fluidity reflects that of the stage. For the reader's convenience, I quote from the first 1703 Tonson edition, rather than later reprints, unless a specific performance tradition is under discussion.

2 A Tragedy Reviv'd: Celebrity Casting and Shakespearean Intertexts

And the Concourse was so great, that several Ladies of the first Rank were excluded for want of room

– Daily Courant, 23 February 1730

The Fair Penitent's performance history really begins with Drury Lane's star-studded 1725 production, featuring Barton Booth as Lothario, Robert Wilks as Altamont, William Mills as Horatio and Anne Oldfield as Calista. Exact performance records are patchy, but we know it was performed at least six times in the 1725–1726 season, starting with a three-night run in November.[8] This is the beginning of a new chapter for *The Fair Penitent*. From this moment it becomes a repertory staple, boasting at least one performance nearly every season between 1725 and 1796, with the result that three hundred and seventeen of the play's known three hundred forty performances follow Drury Lane's 1725 revival.[9] The enthusiasm and public support for this play after 1725 is also seen in the shift in advertising from benefits for (usually lesser) actors or theatrical servants like the box-keeper John Rudd, to performances 'By Their Majesties' Command', such as that for Anne Oldfield's benefit on 19 March 1730 (*Daily Courant*, 18 March 1730). Indeed, by 1730, this once-dusty play was something of a craze: at the beginning of a run in February, the daily playbill boasted 'The Boxes not being sufficient to answer the great Demand for Places, at the particular Desire of several Persons of Quality, the Pit and Boxes will be put together, for their better Accommodation' and warns that 'No Persons to be admitted without printed Tickets' (*Daily Courant*, 19 February 1730). The play was performed again two days later with the same crowd-control measures and an assurance that 'The Tickets that were not receiv'd last Thursday will be taken' but even this was insufficient to meet the popular demand to see *The Fair Penitent* (*Daily Courant*, 21 February 1730). On the following Monday, it was reported that 'On Saturday Night *The Fair Penitent* was Acted again at Drury Lane, where the same Gentleman, who performed on Thursday Night, acted again with great Applause the Part of *Lothario,* which used to be assigned to the celebrated Mr. Booth; and the Concourse was so great, that several Ladies of the first Rank were excluded for want of room' (*Daily Courant*, 23 February 1730). Oldfield's 19 March 1730 benefit, her penultimate performance,[10] was

---

[8] *The London Stage* has identified performances on 12, 13 and 15 November 1725. Further performances took place on 11 December, 19 January 1726 and 8 March 1726 (*LS* 2.2.840–1, 845, 851 and 858).

[9] The exceptions are 1759 and a hiatus between December 1789 and January 1792.

[10] Oldfield would die on 23 October 1730. Her last known performance was Jane Shore on 15 April 1730.

advertised as a change from the current reigning tragedy and Oldfield vehicle *Sophonisba* to *The Fair Penitent* at the request of royalty. That night, Calista's penitence played out in front of the 'King, Queen, Prince of Wales, and three eldest Princesses' (*Universal Spectator*, 21 March 1730). *The Fair Penitent* had arrived, and for the rest of the century it would continue to draw crowds and tears, to be the favourite play of royalty and theatrical celebrities. But this theatrical longevity does not imply interpretive stability. Each actor to take up a role breathed new life and new meaning into the play. Significantly, as new audience favourites took on new roles, those characters too became audience favourites. Tracing the shifting cast lists of the 1720s through 1750s illustrates how *The Fair Penitent*'s affective axis – and interpretation – was altered as celebrity actors stepped into different roles, colouring Rowe's characters with their own celebrity personae and the ghosts of their repertory pasts. Between 1725 and 1742 Rowe's play underwent several significant shifts as audiences were encouraged to focus on (if not sympathise with) Altamont, Lothario and Calista through the performances of the celebrity actors who embodied them.

2.1 Altamont's New-Found Sex Appeal

The first 1725 performance, like the initial 1715 revival, was advertised as occurring 'at the particular Desire of several Ladies of Quality', but the small bill also included cast information. The whole bill reads: 'This present Friday, being the 12th of November, will be Reviv'd, Tragedy call'd, The Fair Penitent. Written by N. Rowe, Esq; late Poet Laureat. Lothario by Mr. Booth, Altamont Mr. Wilks, Horatia [sic] Mr. Mills, Sciolto Mr. Williams, Calista Mrs. Oldfield, Lavinia Mrs Horton' (*Daily Courant*, 12 November 1725). The inclusion of a cast list was not uncommon by 1725, but the order in which they appear is significant. Cast lists illustrate the relative standing of the actors more than the importance of the fictional characters portrayed, but, at the same time, the bigger the actor, the bigger the part seemed: the celebrity performer passed on the unusual interest audiences took in them to the role they played.[11] In the first *Fair Penitent* playbill to include actors' names, the eponymous fair penitent, played by Mrs Thurston, is given top billing, followed by James Quin, who played Horatio (*Daily Courant*, 11 January 1718). In 1730, Horatio is demoted (and accidentally feminised) behind both Booth's Lothario and Wilks's

---

[11] See Roach (2007) for more on the 'abnormal interest' celebrities inspire. For an example of this phenomenon, see David Garrick's repertoire. Garrick frequently took on roles with limited stage time (e.g. Lusigan in Aaron Hill's *Zara* 1736) in an attempt to balance his managerial and acting responsibilities. Being David Garrick, his name topped the bills, leading audiences –and some modern critics – to assume Lusigan was the leading role.

Altamont. Mills did not have the star power of Booth and Wilks,[12] and the allocation and advertising of roles tells us something about their interpretation and reception: Booth and Wilks imbued Lothario and Altamont with their star power and outshone Mills' Horatio, shifting the play's affective axis from Horatio and Altamont's loyal friendship to Altamont and Lothario's deadly enmity.

Oldfield, Booth and Wilks were the greatest theatrical celebrities of the 1720s, so it is no surprise that their interpretation of *The Fair Penitent* should take the town by storm and hold the boards unopposed. Indeed, so great was their command of the play for the rest of the decade (although Booth gave up Lothario in 1727, when a violent illness caused a temporary retirement), that no other theatre even attempted a rival production until 1729, when the new theatre in Goodman's Fields, managed by Thomas Odell, identified *The Fair Penitent* as a potential star vehicle for Henry and Nancy Giffard, new arrivals from Smock Alley, Dublin. Perhaps counterintuitively, the married couple did not play the doomed lovers Lothario and Calista, or even the ideal couple Horatio and Lavinia, but rather the tragically married Altamont and Calista. This casting, however, is not as counterintuitive as it first appears. It makes more visible the character work and interpretive line likely undergirding Drury Lane's production, particularly Robert Wilks's interpretation and embodiment of Altamont. Whereas the pre-1725 productions all made Horatio the male lead, with Thomas Betterton at Drury Lane and then James Quin undertaking the role at Lincoln's Inn Fields, supported by lesser actors as Lothario and Altamont, as we have seen, the 1725 Drury Lane production gave Horatio to John Mills, an actor described as useful rather than talented, and allocated Lothario and Altamont to the company's two romantic leads.[13] Calista was played by the unrivalled Anne Oldfield. The popularity of this trio meant that their *Fair Penitent* was haunted by the ghosts of performances past. In the decade preceding their *Fair Penitent*, Anne Oldfield's characters loved and were beloved by

---

[12] Benjamin Victor summaries Mills's career with a backhanded compliment, calling him 'the most useful actor that ever served a theatre' and Cibber suggests that Wilks 'chose him for his second in many Plays, [rather] than an Actor of perhaps greater skill' (*Apology* 151) perhaps because he lacked Wilks's beauty, having, according to Thomas Davies, 'large features, though not expressive' (*DM* 2.132).

[13] George Powell, the first Lothario, and John Verbruggen, the original Altamont, were not second-tier actors, but they did not have the celebrity of Betterton (indeed, John Verbruggen is now remembered more for his marriage to Susannah Mountfort Verbruggen than for his own acting career – the *ODNB* grants him a mere paragraph at the end of his wife's lengthy biography). Similarly, when the play was revived at LIF, Leigh's Lothario was decidedly inferior to Quin's Horatio: Leigh was described as 'an actor on the stage of no great credit' (Whincop, qtd BDA) and the best the *BDA* can say of him is that he was 'given a few leading roles and a number of solid secondary parts' (*BDA*, vol 9, p. 234). Thomas Smith, the actor playing Altamont, was decidedly second tier, not even meriting snide commentary by contemporaries or later historians.

Booth's and Wilks's in equal measure. In tragedy, Oldfield played Cleopatra to Booth's Antony in *All for Love* (revived 1718), Anna Bullen to Booth's Henry VIII in *Virtue Betray'd* (revived 1725), Andromache to Booth's Pyrrhus in *The Distrest Mother* (1712) and Imoinda to Booth's eponymous Oroonoko (revived 1715); Oldfield played Marcia to Wilk's Juba in *Cato* (1713), Jane Shore to Wilks's Dumont in *Jane Shore* (1714), and the tragic Queen Mary to Wilks's Norfolk in *The Albion Queens; or the Death of Mary Queen of Scotland* (revived 1704).

While Barton Booth's main successes were in tragedy, it was in comedy that both Oldfield and Wilks, to paraphrase their friend Colley Cibber, outdid their usual outdoingness. Wilks and Oldfield created some of the century's most enduring comic couples, and just in the few weeks before they debuted their *Fair Penitent*, audiences could have seen the two together as Mrs Sullen and Archer (*The Beaux Stratagem*, 18 October), the Wanton Wife and Lovemore (*The Amorous Widow*, 23 October), Biddy and Captain Clerimont (*The Tender Husband*, 28 October), and as *The Constant Couple*'s Sir Harry Wildair and Lady Lurewell (9 October). This last was one of the most popular of Oldfield and Wilks's pairings: they appeared together as Lurewell and Wildair at least seventy eight times, a record closely followed by their Marcia and Juba, which they played at least seventy-five times.[14] While Wilks and Oldfield did not always play each other's love interests, the frequency and popularity of their stage partnerships prepared audiences to see the two as well matched, and their stage romance as a play's happy ending. Oldfield and Wilks are a perfect example of 'actors who so frequently appeared together that the ghosted memory of their relationship was carried from production to production in a manner identical to the memory of personal associations' (Carlson, 2001: 93). More importantly for *The Fair Penitent*'s fortunes, Wilks's established repertoire, both with and without Oldfield, built on his line in charismatic, witty, and desirable men. Wilks played the lover in both comedy and tragedy: he was praised for his 'tenderness' in tragedy and his 'distinction of manner, which caused him to be accepted as a model of behaviour' (Murtin, 2004). Wilks's celebrity, stage presence and his performance history all imbued his Altamont with sex appeal, and would focus attention (and sympathy) on his tribulations in love.

Henry Giffard's acting line was similar to Wilks's: he was a handsome, fashionable actor with a flair for comic rakes, and his off-stage marriage to the actress playing Calista added an extra *frisson* to Calista's infidelity and

---

[14] Wilks first created Sir Harry in 1699 opposite Susanna Verbruggen; Oldfield inherited the role after Verbruggen's death in 1704.

Altamont's pain.[15] Familial or conjugal casting was a common tactic to manage audience reactions, especially to depictions of adultery, for example in John Vanbrugh's *The Relapse* (1696), in which Loveless's on-stage adulterous relapse with Berinthia was performed by husband and wife John and Susannah Verbruggen: the shock of witnessing Berinthia's willing seduction was mitigated in performance by the knowledge that Susannah Verbruggen was playing opposite her husband. Conversely, casting the Giffards as Altamont and Calista emphasises, rather than mitigates, Calista's adultery. The Goodman's Fields production further centred the domestic tragedy by casting Henry's brother William Giffard as Calista's father Sciolto. This production also diminished Horatio's significance by giving that role to the unrelated and unknown Philip Huddy, who was making his debut (*BDA*: 8.12). These casting decisions all focused audience attention on Altamont's suffering and lent dramaturgical weight to his claim to be, as in Massinger and Field's *Fatal Dowry*, the play's lead.

The casting patterns of the 1720s recalibrated the play's affective axis, which had previously privileged Betterton's Horatio, by giving more weight to the characters played by the more popular actors. By casting a company's romantic lead as Altamont, audiences are encouraged to feel with and for the betrayed husband. Altamont is made worthy of Sciolto's preference and Calista's love by the authority and charisma of the actor playing him. The dramaturgical effect of Wilks's sex appeal and Henry Gifford's legitimate claim to his Calista's affections is to rebalance the play's tragedy. Encouraging sympathetic engagement with Altamont's pain makes his spurned love for Calista dramatically equivalent to Calista's love for Lothario: in the Oldfield-Wilks-Booth production, *The Fair Penitent* is a love triangle, not (just) a she-tragedy. Altamont's love balances Lothario's cruelty: this helps ensure that audience sympathies are not exhausted with Lothario's death at the end of act four (and may have been the interpretive tweak needed to respond to the audience disaffection with the play's climax as performed in 1703, as noted by Downes). In this reading of the play, Altamont's destruction of his rival is the culmination of his tragedy, rather than any kind of victory. Far from ending the rivalry between the men, Lothario's death unleashes both private and public rebellion, as Lothario's followers riot in the streets and Calista rejects her husband's bed for her dead lover's bier.

With an actor like Wilks or Giffard in the role, Altamont is shown to be not merely the man chosen by Calista's father, but a man worthy of Calista's love;

---

[15] However, if the chronology found in their respective entries in the *Biographical Dictionary of Actors* is reliable, it would appear that Nancy was already living with Henry Giffard and his first wife, her sister Mary, before Mary's death and Henry and Nancy's hasty marriage in 1728 or 1729 (*BDA*, Highfil et al., 6.187, 195).

he is one likely to be admired, if not actually preferred, by audiences trained through previous performances, through the repertory ghosts that each actor carried. When played by an actor like the debonair Wilks or Giffard, audiences can see from the play's opening what Calista is blind to until the very end, when she finally recognises his 'Tenderness' and the 'Graces that adorn [his] Youth' and sighs 'With thee I might have liv'd, for Ages blest, / And dy'd in Peace within thy faithful Arms' (V.194, 195, 197–8). The Goodman's Fields production tries to ensure this affective response through their casting of the comparably unknown (but wonderfully named) William Williams as their Lothario. Whereas Drury Lane offered audiences a near equal choice between rival managers Booth and Wilks, Goodman's Fields's casting of Henry Giffard opposite William Williams nudges audiences away from Lothario and towards Altamont, who is not only 'really' married to Calista, but also the company's rising star and main marquee draw. Endowing Altamont with sex appeal and star power makes Calista's refusal to give up Lothario less sympathetic, and Altamont's tears, rather than Calista's death, the play's tragic climax. This marks a significant shift in affective engagement from the Betterton-Quin years, when Altamont's sorrow merely made dramatic space for Horatio's civic manliness (Wilson, 2012: 64). But, while Horatio's 'sententious speech' may still end the play, the speech itself encourages audiences to feel, like Horatio, for Altamont, the 'injur'd bridegroom' (V.290). Audiences are exhorted to sympathise with Altamont and see his survival as poetic justice.

This invocation of sympathy for Altamont is a fairly short-lived interpretive line, as later celebrity castings centre first Lothario's villainy and then Calista's complicated character. In his *General View of the Stage*, Thomas Wilkes complains that Altamont is 'so clouded by the vivacity of Lothario [and] the spirit of Calista' that 'we have scarcely room to take any notice of him, even when he is on the Stage' (Wilkes, 1759: 24–5). Indeed, Altamont is crowded out of performance, as several of his more sympathetic speeches disappear in mid and late century performances, limiting his stage time and opportunities to engage audience affections. For instance, his nineteen-line soliloquy at the opening of Act IV disappears from performance (and is cut or marked as cut in contemporary editions of the play). Altamont's sorrow in this scene literally sets the stage for Lothario and Calista's tryst: cutting it focuses audiences on Calista's betrayal and Lothario's treachery rather than Altamont's pain. Additional cuts to Altamont's part, including several short speeches in Acts II and III in which he praises Horatio, further erode not only his stage time, but also Horatio's character: by cutting peans to Horatio's virtue, it is easier for audiences to overlook it. Casting and judicious cutting like this reorient audiences away from rational appreciation of Horatio and Lavinia's marital and civic bonds in favour of the Calista-Lothario-Altamont love triangle.[16] Over the course of the century, the ideal couple Horatio and Lavinia become increasingly marginal to the play's public appeal and marketing. In his *General History of the Stage*, the Drury Lane prompter William Rufus Chetwood dismisses Horatio as a 'Monitor' and a 'troublesome Puppy' and relishes the tongue-lashing Oldfield's Calista gives him in Act III, when her 'excellent clear Voice of Passion, her piercing flaming Eye, with Manner and Action suiting' makes both Horatio and the audience 'shrink with Awe' and sends the diminished Horatio scuttling 'into a Mouse-hole' (Chetwood, 1749: 202–3). Cumberland is even more scathing in 1817, condemning Horatio as not just a 'busy-body' who mismanages his interviews with Calista, Lothario and Altamont, but a man who, by stooping to read Calista's private letter, 'can no longer be considered as a man of honour' (Cumberland, 1817: viii). Lavinia endures an even greater diminution of star power: Anne Bracegirdle, who created Lavinia in 1703, is the last first-tier actress to perform the role; it became little more than a useful ingénue part for untried or second-tier actresses, such as Jane Cibber, Theophilus Cibber's first wife, or a Mrs Ramsay, who used Lavinia for her first appearance 'on any stage' (*General Advertiser*, 29 January 1746). Lavinia disappears from reviews, is the ostensibly main character most frequently omitted from the bills, and has the most lines cut in performance. Cumberland mentions her in his Critique only to dismiss her as 'insipid' (Cumberland, 1817: xii) The Oldfield-Booth-Wilks reimagining of *The Fair Penitent* confirmed their characters as the play's leads: their celebrity and audience support permanently shifted the affective impact of the play and all of its characters. From this point on all the dramatic focus was on Calista, Altamont and Lothario.

The success of Oldfield, Wilks and Booth, however, was also a problem for *The Fair Penitent*'s performance history. They were so successful in defining the characters of Calista, Altamont and Lothario that audiences seemed loathe to accept other actors in those roles. After Oldfield's death in 1730, Drury Lane omitted all actors' names in bills for *The Fair Penitent* until spring 1734, when the company's young actors were given a trial. Theophilus Cibber, freshly returned from an actor's mutiny, took on Lothario and young Adam Hallam played Altamont, in pale imitation of Wilks if Thomas Davies's account is to be

---

[16] In his lengthy examen of *The Fair Penitent* for *The Observer* in 1786, Richard Cumberland argues that Horatio and Lothario battle for precedence and that Rowe is, perhaps unwittingly, of the devil's party as he gives Lothario the advantage: 'His high spirit, brilliant qualities and fine person are so described, as to put us in danger of false impressions in his favour, and to set the passions in opposition to the moral of the piece' (275). Of Altamont, he calls it 'impossible for the author of the Fair Penitent to make his Altamont the hero of his tragedy' (275) and charges him with 'indelicacy ... which the poet should have provided against: He marries Calista with the full persuasion of her being averse to the match' (275–6).

believed.[17] *The Fair Penitent*'s performance records for the 1730s show a play popular enough to appear on every stage in every season, but never drawing crowds big enough to sustain repeat performances: these traces suggest a play that audiences wanted to see, but left disappointed, an interpretation supported by the fact that it was recast in part or in whole nearly every year as companies tried, and failed, and tried again to recreate the magic of the Oldfield-Wilks-Booth triumvirate. Bringing the outsized celebrity James Quin (1693–1766) back as Horatio in 1733 (he had last appeared in that role in 1718) may have been an attempt to fill this gap by returning the play to its earlier affective weighting – encouraging audiences to admire Horatio (billed first) before pitying Altamont, sympathising with Calista or appreciating Lothario. But it did not work: not even Quin's celebrity had the power to re-reorient audience's affective engagement with *The Fair Penitent*'s tragedy. Throughout the 1730s, *The Fair Penitent* was a play in search of a stable cast and/or a new generation of stars, which it found in the 1740s.

The next time *The Fair Penitent* would draw crowds was 1741, when David Garrick, whose reinterpretation of Lothario offered audiences a new Shakespearean villain closely modelled on the emerging actor's Richard III. Garrick's villainous Lothario was quickly followed by a new interpretation of Calista by Susannah Arne Cibber, whose established line in suffering wives (on stage and off) and repertory pairing of *The Fair Penitent* with *Romeo and Juliet* encouraged audiences to pity rather than condemn the eponymous heroine. Garrick and Cibber completed the diminution of Altamont as their rising celebrity focused audience attention and emotional engagement even more closely on Lothario and Calista.

2.2 Shakespearean Ghosts I: David Garrick, Richard III and Lothario

On 2 December 1741, the new actor David Garrick, who had rocketed to public acclaim and notice that autumn at Goodman's Fields in the title role of *Richard III*, was granted a benefit in recognition of this success. Rather than reprise Richard, he chose to debut a new role: *The Fair Penitent*'s Lothario. The advance bills for the benefit performance advertised 'Garrick, who perform'd King Richard', thus working to connect Garrick, *Richard III*, and *The Fair Penitent* together in the public consciousness (*Daily Post*, 2 December 1741). Lothario was a savvy choice for Garrick. *The Fair Penitent* was a staple of the

---

[17] 'Mr. Adam Hallam, who, by an imitation of the action of Wilks, especially in a certain peculiar custom of pulling down his ruffles and rolling his stockings, joined to a good degree of diligence, so far gained upon Rich's want of discernment, that he hired him for seven years at a very large Salary. When the term of his engagement was expired, his employer dismissed him, and for the greatest part of his remaining life he was an itinerant actor' (Davies, 1784 v.1, p. 100).

Goodman's Fields company, and Nancy Giffard was a popular Calista. But they had struggled to find a Lothario, replacing William Williams with Denis Delane in 1733, a 'Gentleman who never appeared on any Stage before' in 1736, James Marshall in 1740, and finally Henry Giffard himself traded Altamont for Lothario in April 1741.[18] Garrick could thus step into a role no one owned. Indeed, there was no rival anywhere in London, as Covent Garden had not staged the play since 1739, and Drury Lane's Lothario, William Milward, had left the stage in October 1741. This vacancy gave Garrick scope to claim Lothario, a tactic similar to his choice of Richard III for his debut.[19] But while pragmatic considerations such as these may have nudged Garrick toward Lothario, it proved an inspired dramaturgical choice as well. By pairing Lothario with his Richard III, Garrick's Lothario read as another charismatic villain, wonderfully watchable in his wickedness. Garrick recreated Lothario by imbuing him with the ghost of his Richard III.

When Garrick took on Lothario, his entire repertory history was the role of Richard III. His breakout performance as Shakespeare's twisted tyrant created audience expectations for a tragedy centred on Lothario's machinations: the benefit advertising ensured that all eyes were on Garrick, rather than any of his co-stars. Garrick's Richard III informed not just his acting of Lothario, but also audience reception. The same audiences who flocked to see his Richard came to see his Lothario with the previous performance still fresh in their memories. The *Richard III* performed in the eighteenth century was Colley Cibber's 1699 adaptation, which radically pruned Shakespeare's history play in order to create a tragedy focused on the eponymous villain. In Cibber's adaptation, Richard speaks nearly 40 per cent of the play's lines and is onstage for fifteen of the adaptation's twenty scenes (Stern, 2012). In this *Richard III*, Richard is a Machiavellian character, a puppet master with a talent for moving people to his will, not through violence, even though he opens the play by murdering Edward, but with rhetoric. Richard's Act II wooing of Lady Anne and his Act III wooing of the Lord Mayor give an actor opportunity to portray a range of passions in quick and overlapping succession as Richard demonstrates his seductive powers to audiences both onstage and off. It is a bravura performance designed to showcase an actor's skill, but one that also extends sympathy to the duped parties.

---

[18] *The London Stage* identifies performances on 5 March 1733, 23 March and 3 April 1736, 20 November 1740, and 7 April 1741.

[19] In his *Memoirs of the Life of David Garrick,* Thomas Davies notes the 'an Actor, who, in the first display of his talents, undertakes a principal character, has generally, amongst other difficulties, the prejudices of the audience to struggle with in favour of an established performer. Here, indeed, they were not insurmountable. Cibber, who had been much admired in Richard, had left the stage' (Davies, 1780: 1.44–45).

Cibber sets up the two wooing scenes as performances, watched by other characters, whose amazement at Richard's rhetorical powers of seduction model the audience's intended reaction. Richard, like a good actor, moves almost seamlessly through different passions, stepping from cynicism to sincere love in a single beat. The self-conscious performativity of this wooing is present – and made freshly significant – in Lothario's two seduction scenes as well. In Act I, Lothario describes his prior seduction of Calista to his friend Rossano, who, like the audience, hangs on every luxuriant word. But it is in Act IV that the parallel between the two plays is most powerful. In *Richard III*, Richard demonstrates his villainy by falsely yet apparently sincerely winning Anne's love: 'all of his art, address, grace and refined flattery, is employed to mislead her fancy from contemplation of his victims – substituting his own sufferings, penitence, and despair as objects of her pity' (Martin, 1802: 16). This analysis of Richard III as played by Kemble – who followed many of Garrick's innovations – is also a blueprint for Lothario's second attempt to seduce Calista. Like Richard, Lothario tries to transform his victim's anger to love, and to move her from feeling her own pain to pitying her betrayer's wounded heart:

> Lothario: Hear this, ye Pow'rs, mark how the Fair Deceiver
>   Sadly complains of violated Truth;
>   She calls me false, ev'n She, the faithless She,
>   Whom Day and Night, whom Heav'n and Earth have heard
>   Sighing to vow, and tenderly protest,
>   Ten Thousand times, she wou'd be only mine;
>   And yet; behold, she has giv'n her self away,
>   Fled from my Arms, and wedded to another,
>   Ev'n to the Man whom most I hate on Earth.
>
> – (*FP* IV.i.51–59)

Audiences at Goodman's Fields in 1741, who were familiar with both *Richard III* and *The Fair Penitent*, would recognise and enjoy the points of overlap between the two scenes. Lothario's first words to Calista: 'Weep not my fair' (*FP* IV.i.20) echo Richard's seduction of Anne, in which he strives to turn 'This storm of grief to gentle drops of pity', and 'to take her in her Hearts extreamest hate / With Curses in her mouth, Tears in her Eyes' (*RIII* II.i.66, 265–266). But it is the performativity of each scene that defines both Lothario and Richard. In *Richard III*, Tressel and Lord Stanley watch Richard's assault on Anne: their incredulous commentary creates the necessary critical distance for audiences to recognise Richard's performance as such and avoid being seduced like Anne. Cibber's stage is significantly less crowded than Shakespeare's, but no less overlooked. While Lothario does not similarly set watchers to his tryst with Calista, he does invite them: he knows that the time and place of his meeting are known to Horatio. There is no evidence that Altamont's Act IV soliloquy was cut in 1741, and the speech is intact in contemporary print editions, so audiences would also be aware that Altamont is watching events unfold, he could even be visible to audiences, silently watching Lothario and Calista. He is spurred to step into the scene when Lothario urges 'Love, the poor criminal, whom thou hast doom'd, / Has yet a thousand tender things to plead, / To charm thy rage, and mitigate his fate' (IV.83–85), but he remains silent until Calista cries 'With Altamont complaining for his wrongs – ' (IV.95) which is his cue: he complains by drawing his sword and demanding satisfaction of Lothario. This violence, rather than softer love, was Lothario's stated ambition: 'all I wanted / was some fit messenger to bear the news / to the dull doating husband' (II.ii.246–8). His plan was always to expose Calista, not to seduce her again: Calista, like Anne, was merely a means to an end. Thus, while Lothario loses the duel, he continues to taunt Altamont:

> I conquer'd in my turn, in love I triumph'd.
> Those joys are lodg'd beyond the reach of fate;
> That sweet revenge comes smiling to my thoughts,
> Adorns my fall, and cheers my heart In dying.   [*Dies*
>   (IV.115–118)

His villainy complete, Lothario dies with a smile.

Garrick's Lothario, like his Richard III, was an instant success. He played Lothario at least ten more times in his 1741–1742 season at Goodman's Fields. He would continue to play Lothario 'by particular desire' throughout his career: his last known performance was in 1766.[20] In Garrick's hands, Lothario was a Shakespearean villain; seductively wicked and darkly charismatic. The nature of a repertory company, with its stable cast established in their performative lines, augmented the power of repertory intertexts: the actors playing Richard III and Lady Anne (here Garrick and Nancy Giffard) reprised their partnership as Lothario and Calista. These parallel lines repeated in other companies throughout the century: Garrick and Susannah Cibber repeated this repertory pairing when they acted together at Drury Lane in 1745. But And while Susannah Cibber, like Nancy Giffard before her, initially paired her Calista with her Lady Anne, getting seduced and then destroyed by Garrick's Lothario and his Richard III, by the end of the 1740s, Cibber's performance line – intertwined with her own biography – offered a new intertext and a new interpretation of Calista and *The Fair Penitent*.

---

[20] Garrick does also play Sciolto at least twice, in 1763, but these were both benefit performances (15 March for Susannah Cibber and 8 April for Mary Ann Yates. Both actresses played Calista, and Garrick's role change would have kept the all-star cast without pulling audiences' affective engagement away from the central actress).

2.3 Shakespearean Ghosts 2: Susannah Cibber, Juliet and Calista

Susannah Cibber returned to the London stage in 1742 following a three-year hiatus caused by the public breakdown of her marriage to Theophilus Cibber. Shortly after their marriage in 1734, Theophilus Cibber pimped his wife to one of her fans, William Sloper. When that arrangement no longer sufficed to cover his debts, Theophilus Cibber sued his wife's lover – of his procuring – for criminal conversation (adultery) seeking an extortionate £5000 in damages. He won the case, but as his connivance in the adultery was also proven, he was only awarded a token £10, not even enough to cover his costs. When Susannah, pregnant with Sloper's child, still refused to leave her lover and return to the stage, Theophilus sued Sloper again, seeking £10,000 to cover the loss of Susannah's company and future earnings. Again, it was proven that Theophilus was an unfit husband who had sold his wife and then had the audacity to complain about it. He was awarded a mere 5 per cent of the damages he sought. The trials were humiliating and damaging for Susannah Cibber, who although now separated from Theophilus, was a proven adulteress still living with her lover. When Susannah Cibber decided to return to the stage in 1742, she and her allies managed her return through a number of carefully chosen roles designed to strengthen public opinion in her favour and reinforce her reputation as a woman more sinned against than sinning (McGirr, 2014: 71). She opened her London return on 22 September 1742 with Desdemona, the ultimate in wronged wives. In her first month back on stage, Cibber also played *Richard III*'s Lady Anne, the innocent Indiana in *The Conscious Lovers*, and *The Provok'd Wife*'s Lady Brute, the wife who was so provoked that she could be forgiven for wanting to leave her brutish husband.

At first glance, Calista seems not to fit this pattern. However, by taking on the role of Calista during this comeback season, Cibber was able to make Calista (and herself) appear penitent: Calista's *cri du coeur* 'Nothing but Blood can make the Expiation, / And cleanse the Soul from inbred, deep Pollution' (V.162–3) became an onstage act of penitence by the real and fictional adulteress; one that did not require a similar sacrifice from the popular actress, whose sins were forgiven in the pathos of performance.[21] Throughout the 1742–1743 season, playbills consistently advertised Cibber as 'The Fair Penitent'.[22]

---

[21] Here, another (probably apocryphal) anecdote reinforces this reading. Legend has it that when Cibber sang 'He was Despised' in the 1741 premiere of Handel's *Messiah*, such was the pathos she inspired that the chancellor of St. Patrick's Cathedral, Dr. Patrick Delaney, interrupted the performance to cry out "Woman, for this be all thy sins forgiven thee!" (Davies, 1780: 2:210).

[22] Cibber appeared as 'The Fair Penitent' eight times in the 1742–43 season: 21 and 23 October, 6 November, 10 December 1742, 25 January 1743, 14 March (for her own benefit), 12 April and 20 May 1743. That season, rival productions were mounted at both Drury Lane (with a Mrs

While this advertising strategy was not unique to Cibber, neither Covent Garden nor Lincoln's Inn Fields advertised their Calista as 'fair penitents' that season, perhaps in recognition of Cibber's greater claim. Cibber's public association with adultery – and the public's eagerness to forgive her for it in order to continue enjoying her performances – made the link between Cibber, Calista and penitence stronger and more sympathetic than in other performances, seen for instance in the disjunction between character and actor in Nancy Giffard's performance of Calista opposite her real-life husband.

Cibber's established line in eloquently unhappy wives, like Desdemona and Lady Brute, once again recalibrated audience sympathies (McGirr, 2016). Cibber's performance and personal history worked together to make Calista sympathetic; in Cibber's hands, Calista was unhappy and ill-treated, a victim of male aggression. Established intertexts, like *Richard III*, highlighted Calista's suffering: like Lady Anne, Calista is a victim of tyranny and the male exchange in women for political ends. Sciolto gives Calista to Altamont to cement the bond between the men; he pointedly ignores her hatred of the match, merely urging: 'To Day, I have made a noble Youth thy Husband, / Consider well his Worth, reward his Love, / Be willing to be happy, and thou art so' (III.1.37–39). However, Calista is not willing to be happy, and replies by articulating the wretchedness of all women, who are, like her, 'Thro' ev'ry State of Life the Slaves of Man' (III.i.42). This soliloquy, placed at the play's heart, is an interpretive fulcrum for Calista's character. In Cibber's hands, 'How hard is the Condition of our Sex' is a lament, like her *Messiah* aria 'He was Despised', rather than a call to arms, as it would become for Mary Ann Yates (Section 3). Cibber's soft eloquence demands audiences hear her complaint and focus on her suffering. In a Cibberian delivery, the soliloquy's affective weight falls in the first half, as Calista lists her wrongs, rather than the speech's conclusion that women should 'Shake off this vile Obedience they exact, / And claim an equal Empire o'er the World' (III.i.52–53). However, even here, Calista's speech recommends the Cibberian virtue of passive resistance – to refuse obedience, rather than incite rebellion. Cibber's performance asks audiences to acknowledge and feel injustice, but does not require them to act.

Like Garrick's *Richard III*-inflected Lothario, Cibber's Calista-as-wronged-wife proved irresistibly popular; she would perform it more than sixty times between 1742 and 1764. But while she may have begun playing Calista in dialogue with the miserable Lady Anne, it was another Shakespearean role, and another unhappy

---

Roberts as Calista) and Lincoln's Inn Fields (with Nancy Giffard playing Calista). Neither rival theatre billed their Calista as 'the fair penitent' while Cibber was performing that role.

wife, that would weave itself into Cibber's Calista and the interpretive history of *The Fair Penitent*. On 29 November 1748, Cibber played Juliet in David Garrick's adaptation of her estranged husband's 1744 adaptation of *Romeo and Juliet*. Significantly, Cibber's Juliet followed her Calista. When Cibber's Juliet awakes for the adaptation's extended tomb scene, audiences would have seen and felt echoes of Calista's, as the same actress wept in front of the same scenery over the body of a man she loved more than the one her father wanted her to marry. For Cibber, bringing echoes of Calista, already coded as one of her eloquently unhappy wives, to Juliet encouraged audiences to read Juliet as an (already-doomed) wife, rather than as the naïve child of Theophilus Cibber's adaptation – the most significant change Garrick made when he adapted *Romeo and Juliet* was to age his Juliet from fourteen to eighteen years old, and to reinforce this sense of an adult Juliet by having the thirty-four year old Cibber play her (as opposed to Theophilus's fourteen-year-old daughter, who played Juliet in the original adaptation). But the interplay between Juliet and Calista worked in both directions: Juliet's tomb scene reoriented Calista's, and the 'star-cross'd lovers' of *Romeo and Juliet* offered a more sentimental reading of Calista and Lothario – who, thanks to this new intertextual trace, takes on echoes of Romeo instead of Richard III, turning his rhetoric of seduction into the real thing. The success of *Romeo and Juliet* at mid-century eclipsed *Richard III*'s fame: the 'Romeo Wars' of autumn 1750 were followed by rival productions of *The Fair Penitent*: on 21 January 1751 both Covent Garden and Drury Lane offered *The Fair Penitent*, with the same actors playing both sets of lovers. Whether Cibber's star-crossed Calista softened Garrick's tyrannous Lothario in performance is hard to pin down, but their stage partnership thrived on their complementary differences.[23] Moving audiences from Juliet's bier to Calista's anguished soliloquy over the body of her 'Haughty, Gallant, Gay Lothario' (*FP*.V.37) asked audiences to look at Lothario's corpse anew and see not a villain, but a 'Sight [that] is terrible indeed' (*FP*.V.36). We are, in this moment, invited to feel *with* Calista for the wreck of her love and happiness. Cibber's trademark eloquent unhappiness created a space in which 'the forlorn *Calista*' (V.59) could rave, and mourn and weep, and audiences could weep with and for her – much to the moral consternation of some critics, who felt that the tenderness of this Calista and Lothario played against the improving moral of the play: instead of 'creating a necessary abhorrence of the blemishes that stain them', contemporary performance makes 'Lothario as amiable as possible and the fall of him and Calista highly distressful' (Wilkes, 1759: 25). A Cibberian Calista's

---

[23] The annotation declaring Cibber 'the best Calista' but Barry 'not happy in Lothario' (Rowe, 1763, n.p.) suggests that Garrick's Lothario, if not his Romeo, retained his fierceness. Spranger Barry's Romeo was the softer and more sensuous of the two.

tenderness, coupled with audience desire to forgive her, melts the moral outrage that critics like Thomas Wilkes consider essential, but is unable to impose on either performance or reception.

***

Each new performance of a play changes it; each new actor to embody a role redefines that character. Celebrity casting remakes characters in the image of the celebrities who play them, while the celebrity actors' fame stems in part from their signature roles. Celebrity and repertory worked together to make meaning, reshaping each other in the process. Susannah Cibber's personal history inspired sympathy, which was reinforced through careful choice of repertory. Audiences' feelings for the actress were extended to the characters she played: they pitied and forgave. Actors with strong personal brands, like Robert Wilks or David Garrick, had the power to radically reshape the characters they played. Wilks made audiences see a worthy partner in Altamont, while Garrick's Lothario was a scheming tyrant *and* a seductive lover. These interpretations are all available in Rowe's text; what makes theatre so powerful is the way performance reifies interpretation. An actor embodies their role: the more successful they are, the harder it becomes to imagine any other interpretation. In the late 1720s and again in the 1740s, celebrity actors made the characters of Altamont, Lothario and Calista their own, and in so doing, reshaped *The Fair Penitent*'s meaning as well as its performance history. Eighteenth-century theatre's repertory theatres, with established stars in possession of signature roles for the duration of their careers further cemented their interpretations in the collective understanding. Garrick and Cibber played Lothario and Calista, frequently together, for over twenty years: for a generation of theatre-goers, theirs was the most celebrated, and therefore the most definitive, reading of the play. For a generation of theatre-goers, no other interpretation was imaginable; and the traces of their performances lingered long after the actors had left the stage: 'Mrs Cibber the best Calista' wrote one reader sometime after 1790, confirming their opinion of her interpretation of the role at least 30 years after her last performance. The next chapter explores how actors' performances are reified in print following the fortunes of 'The Calista Mr Rowe drew' in the second half of the eighteenth century.

3 'The Calista Mr Rowe Drew': Picturing Performance

At 5 went into the Pit . . . Mrs Yates is the Callista Mr Rowe drew; Powell did Sciolto well, nor is Bensely a bad Horatio. – 24 October 1767, Sylas Neville MS Diary

As we have seen, the eighteenth-century theatre was an actor's stage: what counted as great theatre was determined not by the quality of the writing, whether new or repertory, but by the quality of the performances. A well-written play might fail to take, and a 'pile of fustian' could keep the boards for weeks, even years, if well enough acted.[24] By mid-century, a repertory canon had been firmly established, and the novelty of a new play was frequently outperformed by the known quantity of an audience favourite such as *The Fair Penitent*. For, as commentators like Sylas Neville show, one of the chief pleasures in a trip to the theatre lay not in admiration of the dramatic text or even *mise en scene*, but in judicious comparison of favourite actors in favourite parts. The mid-century theatregoer was a connoisseur of good acting, and good acting could carry bad writing and even unexciting scenes and costumes. The centrality of an established repertory in this theatrical culture is not evidence of a moribund stage or fiscally or artistically conservative theatrical managements, but rather evidence of the interpretive liveness of that repertory, the astute critical faculties of theatre audiences, and the significance and professionalism of actors, who were establishing the British theatrical canon. As we have seen, actors – not playwrights – made repertory. Actors created the canon we have inherited both by making particular plays popular through their acclaimed performances, and by establishing character and meaning: actors make the repertory through popular acclaim for their performances, and they determine the meaning of that repertory through their acclaimed performances.

***

The second half of the eighteenth century also saw an explosion in print, including new editions and collections of plays. Paratexts, from the *dramatis personae*, which was often updated in new editions to reflect current casts, to the frontispiece or internal illustration depicting a known actor in character further linked the play to performance. Multiple contemporary editions reprinting the same *dramatis personae* and actor portraits reified that particular production: the play as acted was also the play as printed. Notations taken from the prompter's book indicating lines cut in performance further linked text and stage.[25] These paratexts offered readers an interpretive line; the ghosts of performance they carried suggested how the play should be read. After the

---

24   See, for instance, the fortunes of Thomas Francklin's *Earl of Essex* (1766), which was damned as 'a flat insipid plagiarism' and inspired a forty-six-page venomous critique (anon., 1767), but because 'Mrs Yates acted so characteristically, displayed such grandeur of mind, pride of behaviour, resentment of injury, and dignity of action, that the . . . audience was so full of admiration of the unfortunate queen, who, in her last scene, seemed to triumph over all her enemies' (Davies, 1780: 2:95). Yates's performance of Margaret of Anjou made *Margaret of Anjou* The Earl of Essex a success.

25   See, for example, the *Fair Penitent* title page to *Bell's British Theatre* (1797), which reads '*The Fair Penitent*. A TRAGEDY. BY NICHOLAS ROWE, Esq. ADAPTED FOR *THEATRICAL REPRESENTATION*, AS PERFORMED AT THE THEATRES-ROYAL, DRURY-LANE and COVENT-GARDEN. REGULATED FROM THE PROMPT-BOOKS, *By Permission of the Managers*. The Lines distinguished by inverted Commas, are omitted in the Representation'.

loss of perpetual copyright in 1774, canny printers like John Bell created series and anthologies of popular plays, marketed for popular consumption.[26] These new collections were another means of confirming the emerging canon, confidently calling a selection of the repertory Britain's best, 'most celebrated' or, in the case of *The New English Theatre* (1776), the 'most valuable plays which have been acted on the London stage'.[27] The ease with which best slides into valuable reminds us that these series did not create the canon: like editions of plays as acted, they (especially early volumes) reproduced the repertory established in profitable performance. Print and performance were mutually reinforcing: the printed play, whether in a series or published alone, relied on stage presence to attract readers, while the increasing weight of print editions, especially those claiming to identity the 'best' British drama, conferred critical authority on those popular plays.

The increased circulation of print editions of popular dramas was matched by increased circulation of theatrical prints, especially portraits of actors in character. Before the 1770s, as Shearer West details, 'editions of plays were usually either unillustrated, or illustrated by imaginative scenes which recreated the fictional situation rather than a specific stage performance' (West, 1991: 50). We see this in the extra-illustrated and annotated 1763 *Fair Penitent* discussed in Section 1, whose frontispiece is an illustration by Francis Hayman that is strikingly reminiscent of his illustrations of *Pamela* (1740). But after the success of *Bell*'s and similar enterprises, characteristic prints and actor's portraits overtook these more imaginative frontispieces. The actor's prints published in the last quarter of the eighteenth-century do not claim to reproduce stage action with mimetic exactitude, and are, as scholars have shown, as reliant on artistic conventions as theatrical gesture (West, 1991: 57). However, these prints do offer a visual interpretation of a dramatic moment. They illustrate the text not only through artistic license but also by invoking a named actor (with their celebrity persona, repertory ghosts and other attendant baggage) as a hint to how the part *should* be read.

Recent scholarship on actors' portraits, both those commissioned for anthologies like *Bell's British Theatre* and those circulating in print shops, or through collectibles like playing cards or porcelain figurines, has emphasised how actors' portraits worked to transform actors into celebrities.[28] Sarah Siddons was especially good at managing her image in paintings and prints from the early years of her career. But of course it is not just the image of the actor in

---

[26] Bell's series was a popular bargain for middle class book buyers, and Bell's circulating library expanded access even further (Brewer, 1997: 484–8).

[27] See also Thomas Dibdin's *London Theatre: a collection of the most celebrated dramatic pieces, correctly given, from copies used in the theatres* (1814–1818).

[28] See West (1991); Gollapudi (2012); and Halsband (1983).

circulation, but also that of the character they personate, or in John Bell's words, 'a lively DRAMATIC CHARACTER' (1776: 1:4). This circulation made the dramatic character as much a celebrity as it did the actor portraying them. The actor and the character worked together to create meaning; more than just adding visual interest, knowledge of the actor helps the reader interpret the character and vice versa. The celebrity persona of the actor colours reception of the character while the character helps confirm the actor's celebrity. As Bell enthused:

> It has often justly been lamented, that the graces of the actor lived no longer than the Attitude, Breath, and Motion that presented them. – Picture alone can afford any remedy to this unhappy circumstance. The animated figures accompanying the Drama, will aid the audiences of the present excellent performers to recall at any time during life, the pleasures they have received. (1776 I.4)

Bell's justification for his heavily illustrated series – the ephemerality of live theatre – stresses the fact that print and performance reinforce each other. Bell's 'animated figures' were designed to aid the reader's recall of performance and thus aid interpretation by having the reader imagine a particular actor in a particular role (Burnim and Highfill, 1998: 20). Even though many of Bell's portraits are of actors in roles they never played, all of them – both the portraits that do function as fetishes for remembered performance and those that manufacture performance histories – give readers interpretive clues (Gollapudi, 2012: 67). While 'paintings and engravings of actors did not convey the specific nature of performances', they were 'coded responses to the performances' (West, 1991: 26). These images drew on the public's artistic and theatrical literacy to confer meaning and create legible characters. As we saw with the heavily annotated *Fair Penitent* discussed in Section 1, readers *used* their copies of favourite plays, and if a favourite actor's portrait was not included as an *aide memoire*, readers could just paste, stitch or tip them in. Practices such as extra-illustration allowed readers to draw their play text closer to the performance text they remembered or imagined, while annotations offered specific notes on line readings and helped readers hear speeches in the voice of a favourite or celebrated actor. Actor's portraits, whether originally bound with the play or pasted in, did more than lionise the actor depicted: they illustrated the text and created character.

Given these practices, *The Fair Penitent*'s performance history cannot be separated from its print history. It was in print circulation throughout the century, in everything from expensive folios of Rowe's *Works* to (relatively) affordable pocket editions. *The Fair Penitent* was printed and illustrated in anthologies such as *Bell's British Theatre* and *The New English Theatre*, both of which featured *The Fair Penitent* in their first volume of tragedies. The reach of these editions – Bell boasted a circulation of nearly 5,000 copies (Mayes, 1981) – extended the plays' performance histories by bringing the 'dramatic character' of a particular actor's interpretive line into view even for readers who did not see the performance itself. And in the 1770s, when play series and actors' portraits took off, the particular actor most often portrayed in editions of *The Fair Penitent* was Mary Ann Yates, who, while not the only, was certainly the most celebrated Calista between 1760 and 1780. Yates was a celebrity actress with a devoted fan base, which meant using her image made good economic sense. But she was also an actress with a very strong personal brand and performance line. Yates was as famous for her lack of penitence as Susannah Cibber was for her performance of it. Picturing Yates as Calista (and Calista as Yates) taught readers how to (re)interpret that character and offered a radically different reading from that of the Cibber years.

The aptness of Bell's lament about the ephemerality of performance quoted above is demonstrated in the speed with which Yates's portraits were replaced after her death in 1787. When *Bell's British Theatre* was reissued in the 1790s, *The Fair Penitent* was moved to volume three, and Yates's portrait was replaced with one of Ann Merry nee Brunton (1769–1808). *The Fair Penitent* continued to be an actor and audience favourite into the early nineteenth century, but was attracting new criticisms, printed in 'Remarks' and critiques that found fault with the characters' morals, with Rowe's verse, and with audience's continued enjoyment of the play. While Horatio, Altamont, Sciolto and Lothario are all critically examined and found not up to contemporary standards, it is Calista, because she is the title character and because she is sexually impure, who receives the lion's share of criticism (and implicitly, because she is the character most beloved by audiences – there would be no need to censure her otherwise). Actor's portraits and frontispieces from this period contribute to this editorialising in their attempts to picture a Calista who meets both audience and social expectations: the frequent and radical reimagining of Calista in the last quarter of the eighteenth century is a testament to the challenges in balancing the power of celebrity performance with the need to produce a morally improving (or at least not immoral) publication.

3.1 Mary Ann Yates's Rage

Mary Ann Yates was the most celebrated tragedienne of her generation. She succeeded Susannah Cibber in the role of Calista and in the nation's favour: 'G. F. Theatricus' assured London's theatregoers that 'The Loss of Mrs Cibber too must now be less deplored, while Mrs Yates appears' (*Public Advertiser,*

11 March 1766). Mary Ann Yates, however, was not a replica of her predecessor: her Calista was in nearly every respect the opposite of Susannah Cibber's.[29] Where Cibber drooped and hewed the serpentine line of beauty, Yates stood tall and favoured right lines and extended limbs, occupying as much stage space as possible. Where Cibber pleaded, Yates commanded, and where Cibber endured, Yates acted (McGirr, 2018). Where, as we have seen, Susannah Cibber's interpretation of Calista was as another of her eloquently unhappy wives, a victim whose heroic suffering is an act of penitence and expiation, Mary Ann Yates's Calista was, as several contemporary critics commented, not even a little bit penitent. She was instead actively furious. This was Yates's line: she rejected Cibber's soft sadness for her own angular anger. We see this in two near-contemporaneous prints of Yates in the character of Calista: the actor's portrait accompanying *The Fair Penitent* in the first edition of *Bell's British Theatre* (1776) (Figure 1) and a print from 1777, used as a frontispiece in an edition that claimed to represent the play 'as it is acted at the Theatres-Royal in Drury-Lane and Covent-Garden' (Figure 2). Bell's 1776 portrait depicts Yates in the height of contemporary London fashion, seemingly privileging the fashionable actress over the dramatic character, which can only be identified from the caption. However, this artistic choice provides an interpretive key to Calista's character, encouraging readers to see her as their contemporary, not as a character displaced by history and geography.[30] Furthermore, Yates's imperious posture, her steely gaze and strong outstretched arms help the reader imagine the scene and Calista's tone when she cries 'Strike home and I shall bless thee for the blow!' (*FP*, IV.168). The speech alone on the page offers multiple potential readings: it could, for instance, be a supplicating sob, as Calista pleads with her father to end her suffering, as one might imagine Cibber performing it. But this interpretation is negated by the image. Looking at an image of Yates/Calista standing tall and reaching for the sword to guide it 'home', the reader, even a reader unfamiliar with Yates's performance style or reputation, knows that this is not the sob of a supplicant, but rather a command, and stems not from penitence, but from the hauteur of a queen who would rather die than 'groan beneath your Scorn and fierce Upbraidings' (IV.195).

---

[29] Extant playbills suggest Yates played Calista at least ten times between 1760 and 1765, while Cibber played Calista four times. Their equal but opposite attractions in the role can be seen in 1763, when both actresses chose *The Fair Penitent* for their benefit: Cibber on 15 March and Yates on 8 April.

[30] Theatrical costume was in the process of shifting from contemporary fashionable dress to being 'dress'd in the Habits of the Times' as a 1764 playbill for *Jane Shore* advertised. The more historically-accurate dress in the 1777 print shows this trend (*Public Advertiser*, 26 October 1764).

Figure 1 Mrs Yates in the Character of Calista (printed for J. Bell, 1776)
Image courtesy of The Rare Book & Manuscript Library, University of Illinois
at Urbana-Champaign

> Think'st thou I mean to live? to be forgiven?
> Oh! thou hast known but little of *Calista*;
> If thou hadst never heard my Shame, if only
> The midnight Moon, and silent Stars had seen it,
> I wou'd not bear to be reproach'd by them,
> But dig down deep to find a Grave beneath,
> And hide me from their Beams.
>
> (FP IV.127–133)

The actor's portrait served as both an *aide memoire* of the famous actor's performance *and* as an interpretive key to the text. As Shearer West notes, 'in theatrical illustration the aim was not exactitude but impression' (1991: 50). In other words, its function was not to be a mirror of performance but to manage

Mrs Yates in the Character of Calista.

It is but thus, and both are satisfy'd.

Act V. Sc.1.

Publifhed by I.Wenman April 11777.

Figure 2 Mrs Yates in the Character of Calista (printed for J. Wenman, 1777) Image courtesy of The Rare Book & Manuscript Library, University of Illinois at Urbana-Champaign

the reader's engagement with the play that followed by bringing the voice, gesture and character of the pictured actor to the lines on the page. Yates's stern face, her straight back and strong arms show readers that this Calista has both power and agency. This Calista does not droop, but is expansive in her anger. What had been passive unhappiness in Cibber's performance is active rage in Yates's: while prints are static, the portraits of Yates in character imply movement and action, and the quotations chosen to cap the images reinforce this. The 1777 print depicts Yates's Calista turning a dagger on herself. She looks unflinchingly at the blade, rather than beseechingly at her father, and articulates her commitment to ending her life rather than living with shame. Both portraits depict Calista in action, on her feet with arms outstretched, radiating strength: this is how audiences saw and understood Calista's character during Yates's reign as London's leading tragedienne. As Sylas Neville enthused, 'Mrs Yates is the Callista [sic] that Mr Rowe drew' (*LS* 4.3:1285).

Yates's tenure in the role altered its critical reception, focusing attention on the eponymous heroine and her aggressive lack of penitence. Audiences pitied and forgave Cibber's Calista, but Yates's call for expiation was not a request for forgiveness. While the sexually compromised Calista was always, on paper, dangerous and potentially degraded, earlier actresses used their celebrity personae to mitigate or soften Calista's guilt. Yates's Calista rather scorned those who dared to judge her. Thus, while complaints about Calista's character predate Yates's assumption of the role, the volume, number and outraged tone of these complaints greatly increases after 1760.[31] A preface to a 1768 edition of the play warned readers that 'Calista has not the least claim to be called *the Fair Penitent*, which would be better changed to *the Fair Wanton*; for she discovers not one pang of remorse till the last act, and that seems to arise more from the external distress to which she is then exposed, than from any compunctions of conscience' (Rowe, 1768: v). When describing Elizabeth Inchbald's 1770s attempt to portray Calista, James Boaden grouses: 'by the way, [Calista] is no penitent, but an audacious, ungenerous wanton, enlightened only as to her true interests when the lamp of life feebly glimmers to its close' (1833:1:41). *The Theatrical Review* connects this assumption of wanton impenitence with Yates:

> Some have deemed the title of this Tragedy, a Misnomer, because it has been urged, that Calista cannot be considered in the light of a Penitent, as all her anguish even to the last, seems more to arise from a sense of shame than guilt: This objection is not strictly just, but, if it was, a lapse in title is no very considerable error. Pride, and her unhappy passion for Lothario, are her ruling Principles, we confess .... – Mrs. Yates displays great Merit in [Calista], particularly in the imperious and passionate Scenes, but we think she is very defective in those of deep distress; however, there is no Actress at this Theatre, capable of doing the Character half the justice she does. (1772: 1:158–60)

Yates, unlike Cibber, was not known for her ability to make audiences weep in sympathy; 'deep distress' was not in her line. Yet despite this seeming flaw, Yates was considered the only actress to do 'justice' to Calista's character; in large part because Calista's and Yates's characters had become so deeply entwined: her ruling passions are Pride and shame (of being judged) for her unhappy love. Thus, while many actresses performed Calista during Yates's reign, including celebrity actresses

---

[31] Thomas Wilkes is an early critic of Calista's character, complaining that 'her grief does not spring from compunction, but from a variety of passions which she is prevented from gratifying' and goes on to call her 'an ill-judging, irreclaimable prostitute' (1759: 24, 25) – however, his critique may have been coloured by his reading of Rowe's source text, as Beaumelle, unlike Calista, is caught in an adulterous act onstage.

Anne Barry and George Anne Bellamy, it was Yates's performance that was reified in frontispieces and print shops, that was recorded in diaries and theatrical reviews, and that therefore became the definitive interpretation. Barry and Bellamy may have been popular in performance, but their Calistas faded into nothingness when they left the stage.

3.2 Sarah Siddons's Real Anguish

The actress who inherited Calista from Yates blazed brighter than any of her predecessors. Sarah Siddons, even more than Mary Ann Yates, was pictured, described, and otherwise imprinted upon the cultural consciousness. Sarah Siddons expertly used print and visual media to promote and maintain her celebrity persona.[32] This persona was not too far different from Yates's. Both actresses were celebrated for their imperious majesty and queenly hauteur off stage and on stage in characters such as Lady Macbeth and *The Fair Penitent*'s Calista. We see this in an early actor's portrait of Siddons (Figure 3).

Figure 3 Mrs Siddons (printed by J. Macklin, 1783) Image courtesy of The Rare Book & Manuscript Library, University of Illinois at Urbana-Champaign

---

[32] See, among others, West (2004); Nussbaum (2010); and Engel (2011).

The bust pictures Siddons in profile, with a fashionable feathered headpiece and her hair dressed in curls. As in the 1776 portrait of Yates discussed above, Siddons is dressed in contemporary fashion, rather than in character, but her 'characteristic nose' (Engel, 2011: 36) connects Siddons to the 'Roman' Calista even before the eye travels to the quotation below the portrait: 'And What bold Parasites officious Tongue / Shall dare to tax *Calista's* Name with Guilt?' (*FP* III.i.108–9). Calista's haughty response to Horatio serves to identify the bust as a theatrical print, but significantly, this image is captioned simply 'Mrs Siddons' *not* Mrs Siddons as Calista: here, Calista's character is illustrating Siddons, rather than Siddons illustrating Calista.

Siddons's 'diva celebrity' links her to Yates, from whom Siddons inherited both her repertoire and this performance line. But Siddons was not a carbon copy of her predecessor. Siddons's persona and performances blended tropes of majesty and maternity, hauteur and tenderness (Engel, 2011: 30–1).

While Yates's actor portraits were all strikingly similar in body line and affect, the images of Siddons show more variety. Another portrait of Siddons from 1783 highlights Siddons's tenderness, rather than her rage (Figure 4). Whereas the bust depicted Sarah Siddons, this full-length theatrical print depicts Calista as performed by Siddons. Siddons is still dressed fashionably, in a black gown, but the image illustrates the play, rather than Siddons herself. Calista is shown at the beginning of Act V in the middle of her impassioned soliloquy over Lothario's corpse. In her left hand she holds a prayer book open close to her heart. Her right arm is extended over Lothario's body; the hand, fingers outstretched, seems to hesitate between dropping to stroke his face and rising in anguish. Siddons is depicted in profile, eyes averted from Lothario (and the viewer) and raised instead to heaven. The quotation locates the moment depicted as midway through Calista's Act V soliloquy: 'I have more real anguish in my heart / Than all their pedant discipline e'er knew' (*FP* V.i.11–12). This is the moment in which Calista explicitly rejects 'holy Sorrow, and Contrition, / And Penitence' (ll.7–8) as unnatural and incompatible with real feeling. By rejecting the 'Art' (l.8) of Christian doctrine, which teaches readers to perform passions they do not feel, Calista connects herself instead to the art of acting, and implicitly praises Siddons's performance. Calista is like a great actress who really feels the passions she performs; Siddons is a great actress by virtue of her ability to convey Calista's conflicted emotions. She, like Calista, has *real* Anguish in her heart. Throughout her career, Siddons coupled this real anguish, this tenderness, with the queenly assurance that her name was incompatible with guilt. While her Calista was, like Yates's, heroically impenitent, she offered audiences and readers space to pity her deep distress and see heartbreak as well as hardness.

Figure 4 Mrs Siddons in the character of Calista (printed by W. Lowndes, 1783)
Image courtesy of The Rare Book & Manuscript Library, University of Illinois
at Urbana-Champaign

3.3 Performing Penitence

When Bell reissued *The Fair Penitent* in volume three of the second series of his *British Theatre* in 1797, Yates had been dead for a decade. The actress most associated with Calista at that moment was Sarah Siddons, but Bell chose to illustrate *The Fair Penitent* with Ann Merry nee Brunton (1769–1808) instead. Before her marriage, Ann Brunton was a rising and popular actress at Covent Garden, where she was a (largely unsuccessful) foil for Dorothy Jordan's line in romping girls and Sarah Siddons's tragic heroines (Jones, 2013: 201). She played Calista only a few times at Covent Garden, and her last known performance was in 1789. In 1797, she had been off the London stage for five years: she married Robert Merry, better known by his poetic soubriquet *Della Crusca*, in 1791 and left the stage in 1792 when his family raised objections to the 'indelicacy' of her continuing to perform (Russell, 2004). In 1796, the Merrys left Britain altogether

Figure 5 Mrs Merry nee Brunton afterwards Mrs Watson (in the Character of
Calista) (printed for J. Bell, 1797) Image courtesy of The Rare Book &
Manuscript Library, University of Illinois at Urbana-Champaign

and travelled to Philadelphia, where Ann Merry resumed her acting career.[33]
These details suggest that Merry was probably chosen less for her interpretation
of Calista than for her interesting marriage, which coloured reader's engagement
with the print and the play that followed. The handwritten annotation on the 1797
print, noting her marriage and later remarriage, attests to this interest. Ann
Brunton was known for her 'sweet voice', 'expressive eye' and 'spotless reputation' while on stage, whereas her husband capitalised on his 'amorous notoriety'
(Russell, 2004). Surprisingly, the marriage appeared to be a happy one and Robert
Merry a devoted husband: this then, was a Calista who had married her Lothario,
reformed her rake and lived happily ever after.

---

[33] Although she was described as 'the most perfect actress America has ever seen', her Calista was
passed over in silence: 'on the 5th [of July 1801], Mrs Merry played Calista, in *The Fair Penitent*.
The unexpected excellence of Mr. Cooper's Lothario is more vivid in our remembrance than any
other portion of this very perfect exhibition' (Dunlap, 1833: 334, 151).

This 1797 theatrical print shares several characteristics with the 1783 portrait of Siddons as Calista. Merry, like Siddons, is wearing a simple yet fashionable black gown and has one arm folded close to her chest and the other stretching forward. Merry's eyes are likewise lifted to heaven. But there are significant differences as well. Lothario's bier is firmly in the background, and his corpse nowhere to be seen. Her hands, turned up at the wrists, appear to be warding off or pushing away rather than reaching out. And while Sarah Siddons's outstretched arm is, like Mary Ann Yates's, perfectly straight, Ann Brunton Merry's elbow is softly bent, suggesting a more pliable, or at least less rigid Calista, than Yates or Siddons embodied. And where Siddons's portrait is capped with a couplet asserting her impenitence, Merry's points in the other direction. The couplet capping her portrait – 'And you ye glitt'ring, heav'nly Host of Stars, / Hide your Fair Heads in Clouds, or I shall blast you' (*FP* V.240–41) – begins a sentence that ends, four lines later, with Calista stabbing herself as she cries: 'Thus, thus, I set thee free' (V.245). By moving the scene depicted in the frontispiece from the beginning of Act V and Calista's explicit rejection of penitence to almost the end of the play and Calista's act of expiation, the 1797 *Bell*'s anticipates complaints of impenitence and shows Calista atoning, if not amending. This, coupled with Merry's spotless reputation and popular interest in the seeming success of her marriage to a notorious rake, can be read as an effort to restore Calista's pitiable character.[34] Whereas pity and a desire to forgive Susannah Cibber for her sexual faults coloured audience reception of her penitent Calista, Ann Merry was able to inspire pity for Calista through the disjunction between her own happy marriage and Calista's doomed love. Both actresses were known for their Juliets as well as (if not more than) their Calistas: in America Ann Merry was considered 'perhaps the best representative of Juliet that was ever seen or heard' (Dunlap, 1833: 308). Not coincidentally, the actor's portrait of Merry as Calista could, with only a change of quotation, be one of Juliet: the actress's beseeching eyes and tumbling hair show us a very different Calista to the poised, controlled and haughty characterisations of Yates or Siddons. By using a print of an actress who hearkens back to Cibberian softness, Bell offer readers a *Fair Pentient* who is truly penitent, while Merry's spotless reputation attaches to the character of Calista through the celebrity pictured: this Calista is no 'ungenerous wanton' (Boaden, 1833).

A later print of Merry as Calista reinforces this reading. This print (Figure 6) was first published in 1807 and was later used to illustrate *The Fair Penitent* in

---

[34] Hester Thrale Piozzi to Dr. Whaley: 'Do you remember Mr. Merry, whom they called "Della Crusca"? He was of our society; and you said he looked like a sly intriguer; and I thought what a rough husband he would make after having been so smooth a lover to ladies of high quality. Not a bit: a person who knew his whole conduct and course of life in America . . . protests he expired a willing slave to a pretty wife, sister of Lady Craven' (Whalley, 1863: 2:415).

Figure 6 Mrs Merry in the Character of Calista (printed for C. Cooke, 1807)
Image courtesy of The Rare Book & Manuscript Library, University of Illinois
at Urbana-Champaign

Cumberland's (1817) series. This Calista draws on both the Yates-Siddons
tradition of hauteur with Merry's own reputation for sexual propriety. The
print shows Merry in a black empire-waisted muslin gown, with a white veil
in her hair which falls over her arm and drapes to the ground. She is resting her
right hand on a black-clad table, while the left reaches out, fingers slightly
upturned. While depicted facing out, her eyes are following her left hand,
looking towards the decorative frame encasing the quotation meant to cap the
image: 'How didst thou dare to think that I would live a slave to base desires,
and brutal pleasures, to be a wretched wanton for thy leisure' (*FP* IV.76–78).
While the text is furious, the image is not. Merry's face is calm and radiates
sorrow. No one looking at this image could imagine this Calista as an audacious
wanton. Strikingly, the image points to Act V and Lothario's oft-pictured bier,

M^r. BRUNTON & MISS SMITH.
AS ALTAMONT & CALISTA.
Alt. What means thy frantic rage?
Cal. Off! let me go.

Pub^d as the Act directs by J.Roach. Russel Court.Drury Lane.Ap.7.1806.

Figure 7 John Brunton Jr and Miss Smith as Altamont and Calista (printed by
J. Roach 1806) Image courtesy of The Rare Book & Manuscript Library,
University of Illinois at Urbana-Champaign

but the quotation comes from the beginning of Act IV, when Calista meets
Lothario in the gardens. This disjunction is, I suspect, intentional. It works as
a riposte to the 1783 print of Siddons as Calista avowing her real anguish and
explicit rejection of 'Holy Sorrow, and Contrition / and Penitence' (V.25–26).
Merry's Calista has turned away from the table/bier; the image and accompanying quotation suggest that this Calista rejects 'base desires' and is ready to
embrace 'Holy Sorrow'.

The bulk of frontispieces in the last quarter of the century depict the
eponymous fair penitent near Lothario's bier, alerting readers that this
moment – and this relationship – is central to the play's tragedy. Calista's
rage, tenderness and penitence take turns predominating, but the setting

remains the same. A print from 1806 (Figure 7) depicts a different scene and offers readers the most penitent Calista of all. This 1806 print, depicting John Brunton Jr as Altamont and a Miss Smith as Calista, moves the tragic fulcrum from Act V back to the end of Act IV: the scene shows Altamont disarming Calista after he has killed Lothario. The portrait is capped with lines from Altamont and Calista:

> Altamont: What means thy frantic Rage?
> Calista: Off! Let me go
>
> *(FP.* IV. 122–123)

The contrast to Yates's actor portrait in the 1776 edition of *Bell's British Theatre* could not be more stark. Again, Calista's line 'Off! Let me go' is ambiguous on the page, open to a variety of interpretations. One can easily imagine the Yatesean Calista shrugging off Altamont's unwelcome hand and striding forcefully away. But again, the theatrical print curtails interpretive liberties and imposes a reading of the line by linking it to performance and the body of a performer. Miss Smith's Calista is caught by John Brunton's Altamont as she is sinking into a swoon: if he lets her go, she can only complete her fall. This Calista is penitent indeed. Miss Smith, dressed simply in a white muslin gown, averts her eyes from Altamont (and the viewer), hiding her face in her free hand to signify her shame. This print clearly shows the interrelation of artistic conventions and theatrical gesture. Turn of the century rhetorical manuals like Gilbert Austin's *Chironomia* (1806) and Henry Siddons' *Practical Illustrations of Rhetorical Gesture and Action* (1807) articulate the bodily performance of emotion for readers, theatre-goers and amateur spouters (Ritchie, 2012). Austin could have been looking at the contrasting Calistas of Smith and Siddons when describing embodied emotions: 'Shame in the extreme sinks on the knee and covers the eyes' he explains, whereas 'Resignation mixed with desperation stands erect and unmoved, the head thrown back, the eyes turned upward and fixed . . . .A fine instance is seen in . . . Mrs. Siddons' (1806: 489). Readers came to *The Fair Penitent* with sophisticated visual and theatrical literacy. The paratexts including detailed *dramatis personae* and actors' portraits prefacing their copy or copies of the play shaped their reading by recalling performances and performers. The dizzying range of editions available in the last quarter of the century is also a salient reminder that there was never just one *Fair Penitent*. Different performance lines might dominate for a time, but 'the Calista Mr Rowe drew' was as variable as the actresses who played her.

4 Female Lotharios and the Power of Repertory

Not all repertory echoes were beneficial to actor, role or reception. Sometimes the ghosts of past performance intruded unhelpfully, adding unwanted associations to an actor's interpretation of a role or so overfreighting a production with possible allusions that audiences were left unsure if they were meant to laugh or cry. This risk is particularly great when the production, or significant elements of it, are experimental, and the mid-eighteenth century was a period of theatrical experiment. The success of new genre-bending forms such as ballad opera and sentimental comedy opened new interpretive avenues for contemporary performers, while parodies and burlesques paid homage to, even as they mocked, the modes and emotions of heroic- and she-tragedies. The intersection of sentiment and parody, however, created opportunities for confusion. Two unusual productions of *The Fair Penitent* demonstrate both the possibilities of mid-century theatre, and the limitations of gender- and genre-bending performance. Two (in)famous actresses, Charlotte Cibber Charke and Margaret 'Peg' Woffington, turned to *The Fair Penitent* at significant moments in their careers: Charke in 1734, when she first attempted to build her own theatre company and began playing male parts on stage and off; and Woffington in 1753 (and again in 1757), when the established comedienne tried to expand her repertoire and reputation. Both actresses chose to play Lothario rather than Calista, stunt casting designed to transform the play and audiences' emotional engagement with the central characters. Both actresses were known for cross-dressed performances, and this history coloured the interpretation and reception of their respective Lotharios. These other roles, Harry Wildair for Woffington and George Barnwell for Charke, created new intertexts for *The Fair Penitent* and new interpretive lines. While neither production was popular, Charke's Lothario was the more successful of the two because despite being the more radical experiment, it resonated with contemporary tragedies while Woffington's performance pulled against genre conventions. However, both actresses struggled to retain tragic pathos in performance – or at least struggled to retain audience's tragic sympathies – and risked burlesquing their roles and the tragedy as a whole: Woffington's comic rakes and Charke's growing reputation for self-parody may have contributed to audience rejection of a female Lothario.

Charke's and Woffington's female Lotharios created several interpretive challenges for audiences: while travesty roles were not always played for laughs, the cross-dressed actress was a staple of the comic stage, and both Woffington and Charke were best known for their comic performances, all of which would have primed audiences to laugh, rather than cry. Furthermore, while interpretations like David Garrick's highlighted the dramaturgical potential of Lothario, focusing an audience's affective engagement on a character who dies at the end of Act IV risks unmooring the tragedy's affective axis and leaving audiences disengaged or disaffected for the last act. Lothario also rarely commands the stage alone: his character is developed in dialogue as he opposes the wills of Horatio, Altamont and, especially, Calista. It is a role that encourages stage partnerships, rather than a pure star vehicle.

Both actresses brought specific challenges to the role as well. Charke played the outcast villain as a victim in an interpretation that owed as much to her own emerging celebrity persona and family dramas as it did to her choice of intertext. Her repeated repertory pairing of *The Fair Penitent* with *The London Merchant* invited intertextual comparison to Lillo's bourgeois tragedy of female seduction and male victimhood. Charke's Lothario-as-victim turned Calista into a *femme fatale*, reversing the seduction narrative and creating a potentially sympathetic Lothario whose crimes arise from an untenable situation rather than constitutional villainy. However, while her ambition may have been to turn *The Fair Penitent* into a bourgeois tragedy, the cross-dressed performance also replicated elements of the broad farces performed by her Mad Company and other irregular troupes at the Haymarket. This affinity confuses the generic and affective weight of Charke's production and risks ridiculing rather than affirming sensibility. Twenty years after Charke's experiment, Woffington offered Dublin and then London audiences a roistering Lothario who drew from her established line of comic rakes and faux-militants, strutting about in an exaggerated and outdated rakish masculinity. This Lothario-as-lothario also threatened to tip tragedy into farce, and may also have offended audiences used to David Garrick's performance of the role: unlike Charke, Woffington had to contend with both her own performance history and Lothario's, and it would be hard to imagine characters less aligned in the popular imagination than Harry Wildair and Richard III.

4.1 Charke, Lothario and *The London Merchant* (The Tragedy of Lothario)

In the summer of 1734, Charlotte Charke (1713–1760) and her self-proclaimed Mad Company of young players took over the Little Theatre in the Haymarket to 'convert it into a Mad-house' (*LS* 3.1:400).[35] Most advertising for the season is firmly tongue-in-cheek: for instance by 'humbly hop[ing] the Town will be as mad as themselves, and come frequently to see their mad Performances. Which will be madly exhibited, two or three Times a Week, during the Summer

---

[35] N.B. the 1734 *Daily Advertisers* are not part of the Burney Collection, and are lost to contemporary scholarship, so tracking details of the summer season advertising and public/critical response is limited.

Season' (*LS* 3.1:400).[36] The gently mocking tone of these advertisements set audience expectations for audacious yet self-deprecating and playful performances: the company was calling itself mad so that you did not have to. This approach gave audiences permission to laugh at the Mad Company, but also to appreciate them rather than find fault – the audacious 'Nature' of the advertised performances anticipated and defused critique. Charke's summer season was full of mimicry, burlesque, and multi-directional satire, such as her parody of the already-parodic *Beggar's Opera*, which she 'Tragedized' by playing it in Roman dress and treating it as straight neo-classical tragedy, complete with togas: she amplifies the comedy of the original by pretending to take it seriously. However, just as trips to Bedlam evoked pity as well as ridicule, Charke's summer season invited audiences to feel with her characters, and not just laugh at them. We see this even in playful productions like *The Beggar's Opera Tragediz'd*, which, like the original *Beggar's Opera*, was both touching and ridiculous. This overloading of performance with alternating lashings of sentiment and satire was a hallmark of Charke's 1734 season and her emerging celebrity persona.

The year 1734 was a season of gender play on and off stage for Charke, who began developing her offstage identity as Mr Brown this summer (Shevelow, 2005). Before her Mad Season began, Charke played Lucy in an un-tragediz'd *Beggar's Opera* at Lincoln's Inn Fields, but she added to her parody's carnivalesque feel by taking on the role of Macheath: her highwayman was not just dressed in a toga, but also gender-swapped.[37] The female Macheath-in-a-toga is doubly removed from Gay's original parodic figure, and this double-reversal enacts a return with a difference. Thus while wonderfully silly, there is also a serious, or at least, a sentimental side to this comedy: Charke's strategy of (re) creating bathos by suddenly elevating the already bathetically reduced asks the audience to find pathos amidst the bathos, and to honour the big emotions of little people. Charke's parodies take out the sting; they are affectionate rather than biting. Her *Beggar's Opera Tragediz'd* is generic, rather than *ad hominem* satire. It is simultaneously a burlesque, a comic debasement of *The Beggar's Opera*, and a (comic) elevation of the loves and losses of Macheath, Polly and Lucy, whose classical trappings are signifiers of serious drama. By parodying that which is already a parody, Charke levels the highwayman and the hero even

---

[36] A puff inserted in the next day's paper continued the theme: "We hear that the Mad Company at the Hay-Market design to keep up that Character, by performing the Beggar's Opera in Roman Dresses, and exhibiting Hurlothrumbo, in which Mrs. Charke attempts the Character of Lord Flames, and many other Performances of that Nature" (*Daily Journal*, 21 May 1734).

[37] Charke played Lucy at LIF on 23 May, and Macheath at the Haymarket on 3, 4 and 21 June and 17 July 1734.

more effectively than had Gay, but this levelling works in both directions. So while audiences are laughing at the tongue-in-cheek seriousness of a highwayman dressed and intoning as Cicero, Charke is also reversing the direction of Gay's parody: while his *Beggar's Opera* turns prime ministers into pawnbrokers, Charke turns her outlaws into orators – but while ridiculing the very idea at the same time. Charke's multiple layers of parody build an affective loop as audiences find themselves laughing at characters they feel for, and sympathising with characters they laugh at. *The Beggar's Opera Tragediz'd* works as a sentimental satire. It's not a satire of sentimentalism, but rather a piece of theatre that is both sentimental and satiric.

This self-deprecating ridicule – making fun of one's project even while undertaking it – gives the audience permission to laugh at and with the onstage antics while also carving out space for sympathetic engagement. Many of Charke's performances – on stage and in print – toe this line of self-deprecating vulnerability, a characterisation she brings to her self-parodies, such as her performance as Mrs Tragic in her *Art of Management* (1734). In this farcical tragedy/tragic farce, also part of the 1734 summer season, Charke sends up her own actorly ambitions and pretensions to be taken seriously: she was, after all, an actress whose repertoire consisted almost entirely of comic maids at this point in her career. Pretending to be a diva tragedienne both reflected her ambitions – she was trying to start her own company, and cast herself in a number of tragic roles – and an acknowledgment that that character was as far from her established one as it was possible to get. Many of Charke's productions in the 1734 season offer teasing glimpses of the interrelation of farce and tragedy, and offer audiences the opportunity simultaneously ridicule and empathise with the characters she and her company portray. As I will demonstrate, this both/and strategy motivates Charke's gender-swapped *Fair Penitent*, but the generic instability and comic pathos she introduces to Rowe's tragedy prove less easy to contain and direct than in her sentimental satires. While tricking audiences into sympathising with characters they were prepared to laugh at had proven an effective strategy for *The London Merchant* (1731), in that case audiences had been taken by surprise by the pathos of characters taken from the ballad tradition (Hernandez, 2019: 51–2). *The Fair Penitent*'s characters and tragedy was well known by 1734, so introducing new affinities with mock-tragedy and burlesque introduced generic instability rather than epiphany: it undermined rather than illuminated.

Recovering Charke's Lothario and her production of *The Fair Penitent*, for which we have no contemporary reviews, accounts or script, is an act of informed speculation grounded in cross-referencing of other performances by Charke and her circle. Building on my reading of 1734's *The Beggar's*

Opera Tragediz'd and *The Art of Management*, I argue that Charke's *Fair Penitent* also attempted to balance both pathos and bathos, to offer up a protective layer of ridicule which imperfectly covered a sentimental heart. By performatively linking Lothario to George Barnwell, Charke sentimentalises the play's villain and offers a version of wounded masculinity her audience – and herself – may have found compelling. But at the same time, her use of mock-tragic conventions and her own comic persona may have undercut this sentimental Lothario.

The first or outer layer of the Mad Company's *Fair Penitent,* with known performances on 19 June and 21 August 1734, is parody of popular repertoire through broad farce and generic eruptions, creative casting and costume. The company's theatre-as-madhouse conceit suggests a mock-tragic burlesque, similar to Samuel Johnson's *Hurlothrumbo* (1729) or Henry Fielding's *Tom Thumb, a Tragedy* (1730), both of which were part of Charke's own repertoire.[38] But rather than tragedizing a vulgar source text, as the other mock-tragedies do, and even as *The London Merchant* did, Charke here appears to be burlesquing the contemporary tragic repertory, which suggests less affinity with the mock-tragic burlesques of her frequent collaborators at the Haymarket and more with her father's early farces, such his all-male *Rival Queens* of 1710, in which the male comedians were shown 'to the most Ridiculous Advantage' (*LS*, 2.1:226). But Colley Cibber's burlesque of *Rival Queens* was a farcical afterpiece which condensed the five act tragedy into two short acts and was clearly played for maximum laughs. Charke's *Fair Penitent* was a main-piece, and does not appear to have been altered except in the creative casting. This suggests that she may have been inspired not by her father's *Rival Queens*, which predates her birth, but rather by her brother's recent attempt at Lothario: Theophilus Cibber played Lothario for his benefit on 30 March 1734 and reprised the role on the 19 April. Indeed, Theophilus's Lothario was the last one London audiences had seen before Charke's. This is the next potential layer of parody: Charke appropriated several of her brother's signature roles in 1734, including *Henry IV*'s Ancient Pistol, the role most closely associated with Theophilus. But while it might be tempting to assume that her brother was both/either a model for her performances and/or the butt of her ridicule, the fact that Charke continued to perform Lothario throughout her chaotic career, long after the public would

---

[38] A 21 May 1734 advertisement promised *Hurlothrumbo* with Charke as Lord Flame. However, no trace of this performance exists, so it is possible that it was dismissed or not attempted. Charke would mount *Tom Thumb* in 1735, and of course she had experience with both plays from her time as part of her brother's breakaway company at the Haymarket in 1733, where she appeared in *The Opera of Operas*.

have forgotten her brother's performance, suggests that the it was the role, not another actor, that attracted her to *The Fair Penitent*.[39]

An additional element separates Charke's *Fair Penitent* from the mock-tragedies and burlesques discussed above and from other cross-dressed performances, like Woffington's discussed below. Uniquely, Charke's production gender swaps and/or travesties both Lothario and Calista (although not Altamont): Charlotte Charke's Lothario played against a Calista performed by John Roberts, a serious actor best known for his *Answer to Mr Pope's Preface* (1729), in which he defends actors and the art of acting against Pope's critiques of the stage in his edition of Shakespeare. On the surface parodic level, playing both Calista and Lothario in drag burlesques the play and encourages audiences to laugh at the sight of serious John Roberts in petticoats declaiming 'How hard is the condition of our Sex'. A male Calista is inherently ridiculous in this layer, a figure of fun as he struggles with his skirts and speaks in falsetto – a characterisation echoing the comic cross-dressed scenes of Vanbrugh's *The Provok'd Husband*, which always brought down the house. Here, John Roberts would be shown to ridiculous advantage, and his gravitas would add to the hilarity of seeing him in drag. However, gender-swapping Calista, even as burlesque, has broader implications both for her character and that of the female Lothario. A female-bodied Lothario spurning the love of a male-bodied Calista, whether audiences are encouraged to see through their costumes and assumed characters or not may be risible, but it also potentially introduces a new tragic note: the bathos created by the gender reversal opens the door to a different kind of pathos. The gender reversal casts new light on both characters. In her analysis of Woffington's Lothario, Felicity Nussbaum notes that '[w]hen a woman acts Lothario's part, it is not clear whether he is tamed and emasculated, or freed to transgress sexual boundaries' (Nussbaum, 2010: 224). When the female Lothario plays to a male Calista, this question becomes even more urgent, as the role reversals and gender play has doubled. Both Calista and Lothario are unsexed by this cross-gender casting, complicating the play's narrative of seduction and filial (dis)obedience.

By gender-swapping the central couple, Charke reorients the play away from the late heroic of Nicholas Rowe's period and towards contemporary bourgeois tragedy; specifically, towards *The London Merchant*.[40] Charke's programming

---

[39] Records in *The London Stage* and the *Burney Collection* identify at least three benefit performances in irregular theatres in 1744–45: 1 May and 27 June 1744 and 7 February 1745.

[40] For more on the rise of bourgeois tragedy and the stage, see Hernandez, Jean Marsden, *Theatres of Feeling: Affect, Performance, and the Eighteenth-Century Stage* (Cambridge University Press, 2019) and James Noggle, *Unfelt: The Language of Affect in the British Enlightenment* (Cornell University Press, 2020).

strengthens the links between the two plays: *The London Merchant*, with Charke as George Barnwell, immediately preceded *The Fair Penitent* with Charke as Lothario in June. At the end of the season, *The Fair Penitent* was performed as a benefit for John 'Calista' Roberts on the 21st August immediately before Charke played Barnwell again in *The London Merchant* for her own benefit on the 22nd. Therefore, rather than reading *The Fair Penitent* in light of Charke's parodies of parodies, like her *Beggar's Opera Tragediz'd*, her programming encourages us to read *The Fair Penitent* in dialogue with the season's other tragedies, especially *The London Merchant*. The close association with *The London Merchant* asks us to take her *Fair Penitent* seriously, to lay bare her production's sentimental heart.

How does *The Fair Penitent* read in the shadow of *The London Merchant?* By aligning *The Fair Penitent* with *The London Merchant*, Charke sentimentalises, rather than burlesques, Rowe's tragedy. In this layer of performance and interpretation, the male-bodied Calista, rather than a figure of ridicule and disgust, becomes a *femme forte*, or just *forte*. The female-bodied Lothario becomes not a heartless rake or tyrant, but rather, like George Barnwell, a young man who has been betrayed into crime by his unwise love. George Barnwell is the seduced, not the seducer, and the power dynamics between Calista and Lothario within the dramatized action are all of Calista's pursuit of Lothario. Barnwell's innocence bleeds into Lothario's rejection of Calista – a turning away from temptation that ironically hastens the tragedy. Charke's Lothario is thus an attractive object to be pitied; she does not portray him as an active, hypersexualised rake. For while Lothario may boast of his prior off-stage conquest of Calista, the Lothario audiences see is passive and chased/chaste rather than rakish. In other words, reading *The Fair Penitent* against *The London Merchant* offers an answer to Nussbaum's question: in this performance, the female Lothario *is* emasculated and tamed; made safe, but also made sympathetic. In *The London Merchant*, Barnwell's fate is designed to draw tears of pity, both within the play (Thorowgood, Maria) and in the audience: I suggest that Charke plays Lothario similarly to her Barnwell, encouraging audiences to sympathise with both characters. She does this by presenting Lothario as an outcast, even a victim of intergenerational trauma. Rejected by Sciolto, Lothario rejects Calista in turn, destroying the happiness of both.

It is in this rejection that the play's tragedy is found for Charke, who may be haunted by her own difficult relationship with her father (Shevelow, 2005: 75–6). *The Fair Penitent* opens with Altamont and Horatio praising '*Sciolto*'s noble Hand, that rais'd [Altamont] first, / Half dead and drooping o'er [his] Father's Grave' (I.i.9–10). Sciolto, Altamont's 'more than father!' (I.i.18), is the primary focus of the opening scene's effusions of love: after a brief mention of 'this

happy day that gives me my Calista' (I.i.6), she fades from sight and Sciolto
eclipses all. The opening embrace of Sciolto and Altamont is watched from
a distance by Lothario, whose jealousy of Sciolto's preference of Altamont
over him fuels his revenge and destroys his love for Calista:

> I lik'd her, wou'd have marry'd her,
> But that it pleas'd her Father to refuse me,
> To make this Honourable Fool her Husband.
> For which, if I forget him, may the Shame
> I mean to brand his Name with, stick on mine.
>
> (I.i.135–139)

The fraught father–son relationship would no doubt have appealed to Charke,
whose relationship with her own father was famously complex (McGirr, 2016).
By hinging the play's tragedy on Sciolto's rejection of Lothario, rather than
Lothario's betrayal of Calista, Charke refocuses attention away from the adulterous love plot, and on to Sciolto's paternal failings. This intergenerational focus
also retains audience investment in the final act, after Lothario's death removes
him from the action. Act V sees Sciolto struggle with the demands of honour,
civic duty, and paternal love, as he tries and fails to condemn his daughter for her
disobedience, a narrative that the serially disobedient Charke must have relished.
Act V also brings a civic rebellion in Lothario's name to reclaim the honours
denied him in life: Lothario the villain becomes Lothario the martyr.

Charke's 1734 summer season was mostly ignored, and she was back at Drury
Lane playing comic maids and other supporting (female) roles by September. But
Charke also began to add breeches roles, such as *Oroonoko*'s Charlotte Wellman,
to her repertoire in the 1734–1735 season. The Licensing Act of 1737 limited
irregular and experimental theatre and careers like Charke's. But she did keep
returning to the stage throughout her chequered career, and specifically to
Lothario and Barnwell, for instance in 1744, when she was once again without
other employment and had alienated another father figure (Shevelow, 2005: 306).
Charke's return to Lothario at these moments in her own life suggests resonances
with her own gender play as well as her vexed relationship with her father: she,
like Lothario, identified as an outcast victim and felt justified in taking dramatic
revenge. Whereas Susannah Cibber's personal history intertwined with the parts
she played, such as Calista, both to protect her own image and to extend the
sympathy audiences felt for the actress to the characters she played, Charke's lack
of a fanbase meant that her roles were chosen less for the maintenance of a public
image than for Charke's private satisfaction. In moments of personal turmoil,
Charke returned to Lothario and Barnwell, often together. Charke, whose (semi)
autobiographical *Narrative of the Life of Mrs. Charlotte Charke* (1755) speaks

volumes about her feelings of abandonment and victimhood, seems to have considered Lothario a kindred soul.

4.2 Woffington, Wildair and Lothario (The Comedy of Lothario)

Margaret 'Peg' Woffington (1720?–1760) was seen in breeches almost as often as was Charlotte Charke, but there the similarity ends. Woffington was a celebrated beauty and theatrical star almost from her debut, which owed much to her (sexualised) appearance in breeches. Woffington's beauty was inexorably linked to her acting and foregrounded by both her fans and her critics.[41] Her first appearance in London, on 6 November 1740, was a breeches role: Silvia in *The Recruiting Officer*. Her appearance caused a sensation, moving at least one male spectator to effuse in verse:

> When first in *Petticoats* you trod the Stage,
> *Our* sex with *Love* you fired, your *Own* with *Rage;*
> In *Breeches* next, so well you play'd the Cheat,
> The pretty Fellow, and the Rake compleat,
> Each Sex were then with diff'rent Passions mov'd,
> The *Men* grew envious, and the *Women* lov'd.
> (*London Daily Post*, 10 November 1740)

Woffington played Silvia at least four more times in November 1740,[42] in which month she also debuted her travesty performance of *The Constant Couple*'s Sir Harry Wildair. She played Wildair a staggering ten nights in a row from 21 November through 2 December, and at least six more times before the season ended that spring – Sir Harry Wildair was as significant in introducing Woffington to audiences as Richard III had been for David Garrick.[43] She continued to play Wildair throughout her career; his character was not just part of her repertoire, but part of her celebrity persona, as we see in the 1751 *Guide to the Stage*, which dubs her 'pretty Peggy Wildair' throughout. Woffington was celebrated throughout her career for to her ability to be equally seductive, equally pretty, in skirts or breeches. This close association makes Woffington as Lothario seem a sure thing, as it brings her popularity in breeches to a new role, but one that was already a firm audience favourite. Blending novelty with familiarity was basic theatrical economics. And yet, she was

---

[41] "But Peggy is pretty, and must be allow'd an excellent actress" proclaims the anonymous *Guide to the Stage* (1751) only half ironically (p. 27), while a popular broadside claims that "Since WOFFINGTON appear'd to grace the Scene, What Stoic Bosom has not raptur'd been?" qtd. *BDA* 16:212.

[42] *The London Stage* identifies performances on 6, 8, 10, 11 and 19 November 1740 (*LS* 3.2).

[43] *The London Stage* identifies performances on 21, 22, 24, 25, 26, 27, 28, 29 November and 1, 2 December 1740. Further performances were 9, 21 and 29 December 1740, 9 & 24 January, and 3 April 1741 (*LS* 3.2).

poorly received in the role in both Dublin and London.[44] Thomas Davies notes
with impressive understatement that 'she did not meet with the same approba-
tion in the part of Lothario, as in that of Wildair' (Davies, 1784: 1:342). How
and why did such an accomplished performer get this one so wrong?

The most common explanation for Woffington's misfire is to suggest that
she failed to recognise or anticipate changing audience tastes and growing
antipathy to cross-dressed performance[45]; however, this analysis does not
adequately explain the continued popularity of travesty performances, especially in comedy. Felicity Nussbaum and Helen Brooks suggest that the
problem is not simply the gender play of travesty performance, but bringing
that play into a tragedy. Nussbaum argues that 'travesty roles are especially
difficult to sustain in tragedy because there appears to be something inherently amusing in a woman's daring to become a sexually aggressive man,
while a serious female libertine coupling a feigned masculinity with sexual
violence, disquieted the spectators' (Nussbaum, 2010: 25), while Brooks
suggests that while the double-entendre of comedy accommodated, even
capitalised on gender play and the contradictions between the character and
performer's body, tragedy demanded alignment (Brooks, 2014: 78). Initial
reactions to Woffington's performance seem to confirm this, as the Dramatic
Register complains that 'the interest, which the heart naturally takes in the
business of this play, was weakened by our being conscious that a woman was
playing the part' (*Evening Advertiser,* 26–29 March 1757). But this line of
argument erases the long history of tragic actresses appearing in travesty,
from Susannah Mountfort (1690–1720), to Sarah Siddons (1755–1831):
suggesting that the problem of tragic travesty was neither generic nor histor-
ically contingent. Woffington's Lothario appeared in the middle of a long line
of women playing travestied tragic heroes. The distaste expressed in reviews
like the Dramatic Register's may not stem from a general distaste of travestied performance, but rather specific concerns with a woman, and specifically
Peg Woffington, playing the part of Lothario, a villain rather than a hero.
Instead of looking for a change over time argument or a generic answer,
I argue that Woffington's Lothario primarily failed because of the specifics of
The Fair Penitent's plot and performance history and the unfortunate juxta-
position of her Lothario with the ghosts of the comic travesty and breeches

---

[44] She played Lothario at Covent Garden for her benefit on the 24th March 1757 and again on the
22nd April. Despite repeating the role, Woffington's Lothario was not well received. The
immediate response to her performance was a small paragraph weakly complimenting
Woffington as "the prettiest fellow on the stage" (*Evening Advertiser,* 26–29 March 1757).

[45] See Rubery (2021); Nussbaum (2010); and Brooks (2014). Significantly, Woffington performed
in travesty as Wildair in between her two London performances of Lothario.

roles for which Woffington was so justly famous. Whereas Siddons's Hamlet only had to compete with the ghosts of her earlier performances in that role, Woffington's Lothario struggled to coexist with memories of her Wildair and other comic parts. This comic repertoire haunted Woffington's Lothario, making it difficult for audiences to distinguish tragedy from parody, and perhaps more problematically, discolouring both Lothario's and Calista's reception and characterisation. A further, but related, challenge to Woffington's Lothario was found in Drury Lane: David Garrick had been the nation's favourite Lothario since he took up the role in 1741. By 1753 (and still in 1757) his was the reigning interpretation, and any new attempt was evaluated by his lights. Indeed, Elizabeth Inchbald remarked as late as 1806 that 'It is a part so difficult to represent that not more than one performer [Garrick] was ever known to succeed in its delineation' (Inchbald, 1806: 5).[46] Woffington's Lothario, then, had two competing associations: her comic Wildair and Garrick's tragic Lothario-as-Richard III. Woffington's performance fell down between the two.

The centrality of Wildair to Woffington's persona and performance history meant the roistering rake was inevitably invoked whenever Woffington donned breeches. This meant her Lothario would read as a lothario, 'a man who habitually seduces women' (*OED*). This is, of course, a perfectly reasonable interpretation of the role: when audiences first meet Lothario, he is boasting of his seduction of Calista and his power over her. But, as we have seen, this is far from how the play was usually performed, especially since the 1740s, when David Garrick recreated Lothario and Susannah Cibber reinterpreted Calista (see Section 2). Audiences were well aware that while the play is explicit that Lothario is in every way unworthy of Calista's love and callous in his exposure of her, he does not act the libertine within the action of the play: there is no *habitual* seduction; his dramatized behaviour is cruel, but not hypersexualised. Lothario seduces no one during the course of the play; the only passion he indulges in is revenge against those who refused to sanction his love, a point Charke capitalised on with her sentimental Lothario. Garrick's Lothario, too, was less a womaniser than a seductive tyrant: we saw how his Act IV garden scene with Calista mirrored Richard III's seduction of Lady Anne, which itself mirrored Richard's seduction of London, his real love interest. Genoa is Lothario's target in this performance tradition; Calista is just collateral damage.

Part of the success of the Lothario-as-Richard III interpretive line (as well as in Charke's sentimental Lothario) is that it makes Calista's continued love for

---

[46] She goes on to say 'This difficulty would almost raise the hope,–that the beautiful and the base can never combine, expect in the fiction of poetry' (5).

Lothario easy for audiences to understand and even, perhaps, forgive. While he is cruel, he is not unfaithful. Calista, whether the eloquently unhappy wife of the Cibberian tradition or the noble fury of Mary Anne Yates's making, is torn between the equally pressing demands of love and duty. She truly loves Lothario, but her duty to both her father and her state is to enter into the politically expedient marriage her father has arranged; Lothario loves Calista, but her father's animosity keeps them apart. Thus, Calista's continual privileging of the personal over the political may be selfish and certainly leads to death and civil unrest, but her plangent speeches against the tyranny of men who would control both her feelings and her body asks audiences to admire, if not condone, her character. The star-crossed lovers characterisation popularised by Susannah Cibber also mitigates or minimises Lothario's villainy. While his cruelty cannot be excused, audiences are encouraged to fantasise about an alternate dramatic universe in which the two lovers could be happy – like Ann Brunton's marriage to Robert Merry. Importantly for audiences' affective engagement with both Lothario and Calista, Lothario's villainy is situational rather than characteristic.

Woffington's Lothario is thus not only competing with Woffington's own repertoire and its comic expectations, but also audience expectations and *The Fair Penitent*'s established affective axis. The conditions that made Charlotte Charke's gender-swapped bourgeois tragedy acceptable ensured that Woffington's Lothario would fail. By (purposefully or accidentally) aligning her Lothario with her Wildair, Woffington threatened audience enjoyment of the tragic romance of Lothario and Calista. Playing Lothario as a lothario, which Nussbaum calls a 'retrograde masculinity' (193), makes him characteristically, rather than situationally, wicked: there can be no imagined happy ending with such a character in any situation. Indeed, this is where the sentimentalisation noted by Rubery is significant: audiences recoiled not from the idea of a travestied Lothario, but from Woffington's Lothario specifically. By making Lothario both cruel *and* implicitly unfaithful, Calista's continued love becomes inexplicable and inexcusable. A cruel and lustful Lothario also holds no appeal for audiences: there is nothing to inspire either awe or pity in such a character. While a sympathetic Altamont or noble Horatio could cut though this disgust and offer audiences a moral centre to attach to, Woffington, and thus her Lothario, is this production's star attraction: it is her name that tops the bills, her performance audiences are encouraged to focus on, and thus her performance that inspires disgust.

But even if Woffington had been able to expand her mid-century audience's horizon of expectations enough to accept a Lothario who was both cruel and lustful, the stunt casting created additional problems for Woffington and the reception of her *Fair Penitent*. As we have seen, the play is an effective star vehicle for the actress playing Calista, the eponymous fair penitent: Calista is given several opportunities to command the stage and audience's hearts, from her introduction to audiences at the start of Act II through her 'How Hard is the Condition of Our Sex' speech at the play's centre, to her soliloquy on grief at the top of Act V. Garrick played Lothario to great acclaim, but, as his biggest stage moments are in dialogue, he needed to play against his co-stars to develop his character and appeal to audiences, most notably in his Act IV attempt to re-seduce Calista. Garrick's long-term success as Lothario owes much to his long-term stage partnership with Susannah Cibber, whose Calista moved audiences to weep as his Lothario awed them. Their stage partnership complemented each other's strengths, or as Thomas Davies describes it: 'Mr. Garrick and Mrs. Cibber [. . .] were formed by nature for the illustration of each other's talents' (Davies, 1780: 1.85). Woffington's Lothario was at a disadvantage in this respect as well. Rather than a stage partnership of contrasting styles, the similarities between the actresses playing Lothario and Calista, especially the beauty of each, further eroded the distinction between the characters they played. Felicity Nussbaum argues that 'Characters originally written for a male actor and performed by an actress . . . united the rake and his beautiful prey, the victimizer and the victim, in the female body" (2010: 191, 193). This creates 'discomfiture regarding sexual difference' (Nussbaum, 2010: 192) in scenes such as Lothario's Act I description of his off-stage seduction of Calista, in which the actress playing Lothario also reminds audiences of the ravished female body being described. But it creates a different kind of problem when the actress playing Lothario attempts to seduce another actress, when the rake and his beautiful prey share the stage.

We see this most clearly in 1757, when Woffington attempted Lothario twice in quick succession. For her first performance on 24 March, her Lothario played opposite Mrs Gregory's Calista. Mrs Gregory (first name unknown), was, like Woffington, an Irish beauty. She had just returned to Covent Garden from Dublin's Smock Alley for the 1756–1757 season, and was immediately given possession of a number of tragic roles, including *The Distress'd Mother*'s Hermione, *The Mourning Bride*'s Zara and Calista. Her Calista was well received, and when Covent Garden first revived the play in February 1757, it is her name that is advertised to draw a crowd.[47] And draw a crowd she did: the performance was so successful that it was reprised three days later on 23 February and again the next week on the 28th. In 1757, Covent Garden's

---

[47] 'On Monday next will be performed a Tragedy, not acted [here] these four Years, called The FAIR PENITENT. Calista by Mrs. Gregory' (*Public Advertiser*, 19 February 1757).

Fair Penitent belonged to Mrs Gregory, leaving little room for Woffington and her Lothario. It is therefore surprising – or perhaps not – that Mrs Gregory was replaced as Calista for Woffington's second attempt at Lothario on 22 April. For this performance, a Mrs Hamilton – probably Sarah Hamilton, Nancy Giffard's sister – played Calista. Mrs Hamilton was far less of a rival than Mrs Gregory and could be counted on to not outshine her stage partner. However, regardless of her Calista, Woffington's Lothario failed to seduce audiences.

The only contemporary notice of Woffington's London Lothario to survive is a tiny paragraph in *The Evening Advertiser*. Where Woodward's benefit performance the same night merited more than a column of rapturous praise, Woffington's received a scant two sentences. While still 'the prettiest fellow on the stage', praise for her performance is limited: 'we must say that Mrs. Woffington takes off her hat, draws her sword, fights and dies with such an elegant gallantry' (*Evening Advertiser*, 26–29 March 1757). Conspicuously absent in this account is her power of seduction, and given that seduction was Woffington's stock-in-trade, this is a glaring omission. West Digges, the Altamont to her Dublin Lothario, carped that 'she neither had spirit nor figure for the part. All that warm luxuriousness of description, which so strongly marks what a Lothario should be, came from her with finical delicacy, that, while it offended the ear, insulted the understanding' (Foot, 1811: 82). Digges focuses his complaints about his co-star on her failure to seduce, to be a worthy rival to his Altamont. While actors' cavils about their rivals – and Digges, who was something of a lothario himself, surely saw Woffington usurping Lothario as competition – should be viewed with some scepticism, his complaints about Woffington's delivery echo the faint praise for Woffington's physicality seen in the *Evening Advertiser*. Both the critique and the back-handed compliment stress the generic, rather than gender, instability Woffington brings to Lothario. The comic Wildair can indulge in 'elegant gallantry', but this mode is too light for tragedy. 'Delicacy' is a comic touch; Lothario's passions need weight to balance Calista's and drive the play's catastrophe. A finical delivery is effeminate and over-mannered, but most especially it is comic: a tragic villain can be many things, but he cannot be fussy. Just as Charke's Lothario's proximity to farce destabilised her sentimental interpretation, Woffington's Lothario's proximity to the comic Wildair diminishes Lothario and turns his rage into a joke.

Woffington was the last actress to travesty Lothario. Her failure in the part exposes the limitations of an actor's ability to recreate a role and radically shift a play's performance history. Just as neither actors nor playwrights can fully direct audience reactions, repertory ghosts cannot be controlled or even chosen. And while much of Woffington's and Charke's failures can be attributed to generic instability, gender plays its part. Woffington's and Charke's decisions to travesty *villainy* was a far greater affront to gender norms than playing a tragic hero would have been: Charke's limited success stemmed at least in part from her characterisation of a Lothario who was more victim than villain, and could be seen as a potential object of pity, not disgust. The success of Woffington's Wildair owed much to Robert Wilks's creation of that character as a reformable and sociable, rather than aggressive, rake: had she followed Wilks's cue with *The Fair Penitent* and chosen to travesty Altamont, she may have found success. Bringing her trademark prettiness to Altamont would have imbued that character with more dramatic appeal and hearkened back to the 1720s performances that encouraged audiences to feel pity for the betrayed husband and amazement at Calista's blindness. A female-bodied tragic victim/hero does not stretch the audience's horizon of expectations too far: indeed, Altamont, described in (an oft-cut line) as 'kind as the softest Virgin of our Sex' (*FP* II.i.14) is an ideal role to travesty. Characteristics such as naivety, loyalty and filial devotion that made him a challenging part for actors map easily onto female gender roles. A female-bodied Altamont could make audiences weep and love him. But Woffington was not interested in Altamont: her choice to play Lothario instead tells how successful David Garrick had been in making Lothario the play's male lead and romantic interest. She chose Lothario because by mid-century he and Calista *were* the play's tragedy.

***

Theatre is the most ephemeral of art forms, largely disappearing each time the curtain drops and being made anew and differently each time the curtain rises again. However, it is never a blank slate. Traces – ghosts – of past performances and performers haunt subsequent productions, while theatre-goers bring their own associations and expectations to performance. Charlotte Charke's and Peg Woffington's attempts to travesty Lothario show the limits to an actor's ability to redefine a role or radically revise a play's significance. Woffington's Lothario was thwarted by both her own history of playing pretty fellows and audience expectations of a Lothario who was dangerous rather than merely desirable. Woffington's performance was haunted by Wilks – but in the wrong role. It was also haunted by Garrick's rival performance of Lothario. The more popular *The Fair Penitent* became, the more an audience's horizon of expectations was hemmed in: celebrated performers 'owned' the roles, not just in their own company, but in the popular imagination as well. Celebrity performances were reified in print and image, in memoirs and anecdote. Readers conjured up the voices of these celebrated performers as they read, recreating intonation, emphasis and accent. Deviation from these expectations led to disappointment or disgust.

By the beginning of the nineteenth century, *The Fair Penitent* was still a repertory staple. Some critics grumbled that Rowe's verse was old-fashioned, but it remained popular with audiences and actors, both professional and amateur. *The Fair Penitent*'s theatrical longevity is directly linked to Rowe's adaptation strategy of emphasizing passions rather than plot. This focus on affective bonds allowed actors to redefine them and the characters they played through performance as they embodied different emotions, from shame to resignation, penitence to fury. This flexibility meant that *The Fair Penitent* and its characters could change with, anticipate or sometimes challenge audience expectations, but it was also hampered by this very success: Oldfield, Wilkes and Booth saved *The Fair Penitent* from obscurity, but also made audiences reject other performers. The rash of new print editions in the last quarter of the eighteenth century advertised the play's universal appeal and extended the reach of popular performances, but also reified those performances and interpretive lines.

Like most eighteenth-century drama, *The Fair Penitent* fell out of favour in the second half of the nineteenth century. Perhaps it has been off the boards long enough for its repertory ghosts to settle and the time is ripe to revive a tragedy called *The Fair Penitent*.

Appendix A: *The Fair Penitent* 1703–1800 London Performance Calendar

Date	Theatre
Spring 1703	Lincoln's Inn Fields
Spring 1703	Lincoln's Inn Fields
Spring 1703	Lincoln's Inn Fields
8 June 1703	Lincoln's Inn Fields
18 August 1715	Lincoln's Inn Fields
23 August 1715	Lincoln's Inn Fields
3 November 1715	Lincoln's Inn Fields
7 April 1716	Lincoln's Inn Fields
11 January 1718	Lincoln's Inn Fields
16 January 1718	Lincoln's Inn Fields
15 March 1718	Lincoln's Inn Fields
20 March 1719	Coignard's Great Room
11 August 1719	Drury Lane
14 June 1720	Drury Lane
2 June 1721	Drury Lane
16 December 1723	Little Theatre, Haymarket
17 December 1723	Little Theatre, Haymarket
3 January 1724	Little Theatre, Haymarket
12 March 1724	Little Theatre, Haymarket
12 November 1725	Drury Lane
13 November 1725	Drury Lane
15 November 1725	Drury Lane
11 December 1725	Drury Lane
19 January 1726	Drury Lane
8 March 1726	Drury Lane
8 September 1726	Drury Lane
11 March 1727	Drury Lane
11 April 1727	Drury Lane
9 December 1727	Drury Lane
2 May 1728	Drury Lane
22 October 1728	Drury Lane

(cont.)

Date	Theatre
17 December 1728	Drury Lane
11 February 1729	Drury Lane
25 March 1729	Drury Lane
8 December 1729	Goodman's Fields
20 December 1729	Drury Lane
15 January 1730	Goodman's Fields
24 January 1730	Goodman's Fields
19 February 1730	Drury Lane
21 February 1730	Drury Lane
19 March 1730	Drury Lane
27 May 1730	Goodman's Fields
7 July 1730	Little Theatre, Haymarket
27 October 1730	Goodman's Fields
5 December 1730	Drury Lane
7 December 1730	Little Theatre, Haymarket
22 January 1731	Goodman's Fields
29 April 1731	Goodman's Fields
21 June 1731	Windmill Hill
12 October 1731	Drury Lane
21 March 1732	Drury Lane
14 September 1732	Drury Lane
17 April 1733	Covent Garden
12 July 1733	Little Theatre, Haymarket
5 March 1733	Goodman's Fields
30 March 1734	Drury Lane
19 April 1734	Drury Lane
19 June 1734	Little Theatre, Haymarket
21 August 1734	Little Theatre, Haymarket
2 September 1734	Red Lion Street
18 September 1735	York Buildings
15 March 1736	Covent Garden
23 March 1736	Goodman's Fields
3 April 1736	Goodman's Fields
15 April 1736	Covent Garden
31 January 1737	York Buildings
24 February 1737	Covent Garden
2 April 1737	Covent Garden

(cont.)

Date	Theatre
15 November 1737	Covent Garden
3 February 1738	Covent Garden
29 April 1738	Drury Lane
18 November 1738	Covent Garden
27 January 1739	Covent Garden
6 October 1739	Covent Garden
3 November 1739	Drury Lane
27 March 1740	Drury Lane
20 November 1740	Goodman's Fields
7 April 1741	Goodman's Fields
16 May 1741	James St
2 December 1741	Goodman's Fields
3 December 1741	Goodman's Fields
12 December 1741	Goodman's Fields
28 December 1741	Goodman's Fields
16 January 1742	Goodman's Fields
22 January 1742	Goodman's Fields
11 February 1742	Goodman's Fields
22 February 1742	Goodman's Fields
27 February 1742	Goodman's Fields
19 April 1742	Goodman's Fields
24 May 1742	Goodman's Fields
21 October 1742	Covent Garden
23 October 1742	Covent Garden
6 November 1742	Covent Garden
10 December 1742	Covent Garden
21 January 1743	Lincoln's Inn Fields
25 January 1743	Covent Garden
8 March 1743	Lincoln's Inn Fields
14 March 1743	Covent Garden
24 March 1743	Drury Lane
12 April 1743	Covent Garden
18 April 1743	DRURY LANE
20 May 1743	Covent Garden
20 December 1743	Drury Lane
7 February 1744	Covent Garden
28 March 1744	James St

(cont.)

Date	Theatre
29 March 1744	Covent Garden
21 April 1744	Drury Lane
11 June 1744	May Fair
28 September 1744	Covent Garden
20 October 1744	Drury Lane
31 October 1744	Drury Lane
24 January 1745	Goodman's Fields
7 February 1745	Drury Lane
8 March 1745	James St
11 March 1745	Drury Lane
6 April 1745	Drury Lane
30 April 1745	Drury Lane
6 May 1745	Goodman's Fields
12 December 1745	Drury Lane
26 December 1745	James St
29 January 1746	Drury Lane
14 November 1746	Covent Garden
15 November 1746	Covent Garden
19 November 1746	Covent Garden
20 November 1746	Covent Garden
21 November 1746	Covent Garden
22 November 1746	Covent Garden
27 November 1746	Covent Garden
29 November 1746	Covent Garden
1 December 1746	Covent Garden
15 December 1746	Covent Garden
31 December 1745	Goodman's Fields
30 March 1747	Covent Garden
11 April 1747	Goodman's Fields
07 May 1747	Covent Garden
27 May 1747	Covent Garden
1 February 1748	Drury Lane
2 February 1748	Drury Lane
4 February 1748	Drury Lane
6 February 1748	Drury Lane
22 March 1748	Drury Lane
26 April 1748	Drury Lane

(cont.)

Date	Theatre
4 July 1748	Southwark
10 October 1748	Covent Garden
12 October 1748	Covent Garden
22 October 1748	Drury Lane
24 November 1748	Drury Lane
24 January 1749	Drury Lane
27 February 1749	Drury Lane
6 March 1749	Covent Garden
31 March 1749	Drury Lane
18 April 1749	Haymarket
3 July 1749	James St
21 October 1749	Drury Lane
26 October 1749	Haymarket
25 November 1749	Drury Lane
6 December 1749	Drury Lane
20 March 1750	Covent Garden
22 March 1750	Drury Lane
20 August 1750	New Wells, Shepherd's Market
10 November 1750	Haymarket
28 November 1750	Drury Lane
19 January 1751	Covent Garden
21 January 1751	Covent Garden
21 January 1751	Drury Lane
23 January 1751	Covent Garden
31 January 1751	Covent Garden
26 April 1751	Drury Lane
15 May 1751	Covent Garden
8 November 1751	Drury Lane
9 November 1751	Drury Lane
11 November 1751	Drury Lane
15 November 1751	Drury Lane
22 November 1751	Drury Lane
20 December 1751	Haymarket
23 December 1751	Drury Lane
24 April 1752	Covent Garden
13 May 1752	Covent Garden
11 October 1752	Drury Lane

(cont.)

Date	Theatre
7 November 1752	Drury Lane
22 November 1752	Covent Garden
1 February 1753	Drury Lane
15 February 1753	Covent Garden
24 March 1753	Covent Garden
26 April 1753	Drury Lane
27 April 1753	Covent Garden
31 October 1753	Drury Lane
3 November 1753	Drury Lane
30 November 1753	Covent Garden
31 December 1753	Hickford's
2 January 1753	Hickford's
4 January 1754	Drury Lane
28 March 1754	Drury Lane
29 April 1754	Covent Garden
6 November 1754	Drury Lane
14 May 1755	Drury Lane
12 January 1756	Drury Lane
3 April 1756	Drury Lane
23 November 1756	Drury Lane
21 February 1757	Covent Garden
24 February 1757	Covent Garden
28 February 1757	Covent Garden
24 March 1757	Covent Garden
22 April 1757	Covent Garden
12 April 1758	Covent Garden
11 April 1760	Drury Lane
20 November 1760	Drury Lane
29 November 1760	Drury Lane
4 December 1760	Drury Lane
6 December 1760	Drury Lane
19 December 1760	Drury Lane
2 January 1761	Drury Lane
30 March 1761	Drury Lane
27 March 1762	Covent Garden
15 March 1763	Drury Lane
8 April 1763	Drury Lane

(cont.)

Date	Theatre
9 April 1764	Drury Lane
17 November 1764	Drury Lane
21 November 1764	Drury Lane
7 March 1765	Drury Lane
28 March 1765	Drury Lane
2 May 1765	Drury Lane
15 October 1765	Drury Lane
16 October 1765	Drury Lane
19 October 1765	Drury Lane
30 April 1766	Haymarket
15 September 1766	King's
16 October 1766	Drury Lane
7 November 1766	Covent Garden
11 November 1766	Covent Garden
13 November 1766	Covent Garden
15 November 1766	Drury Lane
2 December 1766	Covent Garden
8 December 1766	Drury Lane
27 April 1767	Covent Garden
28 April 1767	Drury Lane
7 September 1767	Haymarket
22 October 1767	Covent Garden
24 October 1767	Covent Garden
20 November 1767	Covent Garden
7 December 1767	Covent Garden
12 October 1768	Covent Garden
18 March 1769	Drury Lane
19 April 1769	Drury Lane
4 May 1769	Covent Garden
11 October 1769	Drury Lane
11 November 1769	Drury Lane
6 January 1770	Drury Lane
21 April 1770	Drury Lane
9 July 1770	Haymarket
13 July 1770	Haymarket
18 July 1770	Haymarket
30 July 1770	Haymarket

(cont.)

Date	Theatre
1 September 1770	Haymarket
20 October 1770	Drury Lane
27 October 1770	Drury Lane
15 November 1770	Covent Garden
19 November 1770	Covent Garden
16 January 1771	Covent Garden
26 January 1771	Haymarket
26 April 1771	Drury Lane
2 November 1771	Covent Garden
12 November 1771	Drury Lane
17 March 1772	Covent Garden
6 October 1772	Drury Lane
5 January 1773	Drury Lane
4 May 1773	Drury Lane
26 October 1773	Drury Lane
26 February 1774	Covent Garden
1 March 1774	Covent Garden
5 March 1774	Covent Garden
10 March 1774	Covent Garden
11 February 1775	Covent Garden
14 February 1775	Covent Garden
28 October 1775	Drury Lane
10 November 1775	Covent Garden
16 January 1776	Drury Lane
24 April 1776	Covent Garden
29 April 1776	Covent Garden
8 May 1776	Covent Garden
3 October 1776	Drury Lane
18 June 1777	China Hall, Rotherhithe
16 February 1778	Covent Garden
6 April 1779	Covent Garden
14 April 1779	Covent Garden
4 October 1779	Covent Garden
March 1780	China Hall, Rotherhithe
18 October 1780	Covent Garden
2 January 1781	Covent Garden
12 March 1781	Covent Garden

(cont.)

Date	Theatre
27 March 1781	Crown Inn, Islington
1 January 1782	Covent Garden
26 August 1782	Haymarket
2 September 1782	Haymarket
27 September 1782	Covent Garden
29 November 1782	Drury Lane
2 December 1782	Drury Lane
6 December 1782	Drury Lane
23 December 1782	Drury Lane
30 December 1782	Haymarket
4 January 1783	Drury Lane
14 January 1783	Drury Lane
20 January 1783	Drury Lane
10 February 1783	Drury Lane
17 February 1783	Covent Garden
21 February 1783	Drury Lane
28 February 1783	Drury Lane
22 March 1783	Drury Lane
5 April 1783	Drury Lane
1 May 1783	Drury Lane
22 May 1783	Drury Lane
21 October 1783	Drury Lane
3 January 1784	Covent Garden
10 January 1784	Covent Garden
24 February 1784	Drury Lane
16 November 1784	Drury Lane
12 April 1785	Covent Garden
2 May 1785	Covent Garden
27 July 1785	Windsor Castle Inn, Hammersmith
15 February 1786	Drury Lane
18 November 1786	Drury Lane
27 November 1786	Covent Garden
29 December 1786	Covent Garden
5 January 1787	Drury Lane
16 April 1787	Drury Lane
11 November 1788	Drury Lane
14 December 1789	Covent Garden

Appendix A

(cont.)

Date	Theatre
31 January 1792	Drury Lane at King's
3 November 1792	Covent Garden
23 April 1793	Drury Lane at the Haymarket
18 February 1794	Covent Garden
20 February 1794	Covent Garden
8 November 1794	Covent Garden
17 November 1794	Covent Garden
26 December 1794	Covent Garden
3 March 1795	Drury Lane
6 November 1795	Covent Garden
23 November 1796	Drury Lane
14 November 1799	Covent Garden

References

The Author of Helen of Glenross [attrib. H. Martin], 1802. *Remarks on Mr. John Kemble's Performance of Hamlet and Richard the Third*. London: G. and J. Robinson.

1797. *Ann Brunton Merry as Calista in "The Fair Penitent"*. London: J. Bell.

Anon., 1703a. Advertisements and Notices. *Post Boy*, 13–16 March, p. 2.

Anon., 1703b. Advertisements and Notices. *Post Boy*, 4–6 March, p. 2.

Anon., 1715. News. *Daily Courant*, 18 August.

Anon., 1718. Advertisements and Notices. *Daily Courant*, 11 January, p. 2.

Anon., 1725. Advertisements and Notices. *Daily Courant*, 12 November.

Anon., 1730a. Advertisements and Notices. *Daily Courant*, 30 March, p. 2.

Anon., 1730b. News. *Daily Courant*, 19 February, p. 2.

Anon., 1730c. News. *Daily Courant*, 21 February, p. 2.

Anon., 1730d. News. *Daily Courant*, 23 February, p. 2.

Anon., 1730e. News. *Universal Spectator and Weekly Journal*, 21 March, p. 2.

Anon., 1734. News. *Daily Journal*, 21 May, p. 1.

Anon., 1740. Advertisements and Notices. *London Daily Post and General Advertiser*, 10 November, p. 2.

Anon., 1741. Advertisements and Notices. *London Daily Post and General Advertiser*, 2 December, p. 2.

Anon., 1746. Advertisements and Notices. *General Advertiser*, 29 January.

Anon., 1751. *A Guide to the Stage: or, Select Instructions and Precedents from the Best Authorities towards Forming a Polite Audience; with Some Account of the Players &c*. London: D. Job.

Anon., 1757a. Advertisements and Notices. *Public Advertiser*, 19 February, p. 2.

Anon., 1757b. News. *Evening Advertiser*, 29 March, p. 2.

Anon., 1757c. News. *Evening Advertiser*, 26–29 March, p. 2.

Anon., 1764. Advertisements and Notices. *Public Advertiser*, 26 October.

Anon., 1766. News. *Public Advertiser*, 11 March.

Anon., 1767. *A Letter from the Rope-Dancing Monkey in the Hay-Market, to the Acting Monkey of Drury-Lane, on the Earl of Warwick*. London: J. Pridden.

Anon., 1776–8. *Bell's British Theatre: Consisting of the Most Esteemed English Plays*. London: J. Bell.

Anon., 1776–7. *New English Theatre: Containing the Most Valuable Plays Which Have Been Acted on the London Stage*. London: J. Rivington.

Anon., 1791. Remarks on the Fair Penitent. In: *The Fair Penitent: A Tragedy, Adapted for Theatrical Representation. Regulated from the Prompt-Books.* London: John Bell, p. iii.

Avery, E. L., ed., 1960. *The London Stage 1660–1800.* Carbondale: Southern Illinois University Press.

Boaden, J., 1833. *Memoirs of Mrs. Inchbald.* London: Richard Bentley.

Brewer, J., 1997. *Pleasures of the Imagination.* New York: Farrar.

Brooks, H. E., 2014. *Actresses, Gender and the Eighteenth-Century Stage.* Basingstoke: Palgrave.

Burnim, K. & Highfill, P., 1998. *John Bell: Patron of British Theatrical Portraiture.* Carbondale: Southern Illinois University Press.

Carlson, M., 2001. *The Haunted Stage: Theatre as Memory Machine.* Ann Arbor: University of Michigan Press.

Charke, C., 1755. *Narrative of the Life of Mrs. Charlotte Charke.* London: W. Reeve, A. Dodd, and E. Cook.

Chetwood, W. R., 1749. *A General History of the Stage . . .. With the Memoirs of Most of the Principal Performers that Have Appeared on the English and Irish Stage for These Last Fifty Years.* London: W. Owen.

Cibber, C., 1740. *An Apology for the Life of Mr Colley Cibber.* 2nd ed. London: W. Lewis.

Cibber, C. & and Shakespeare, W., 1700. *The Tragical History of King Richard III.* London: B. Lintott.

Cumberland, R., 1786. *The Observer: Being a Collection of Moral, Literary and Familiar Essays.* London: C. Dilly.

Cumberland, R., 1817. Critique of the Fair Penitent. In: R. Cumberland, ed., *British Drama, a Collection of the Most Esteemed Dramatic Productions, with Biography of the Respective Authors; and a Critique on Each Play.* London: C. Cooke, pp. x–xiii.

Davies, T., 1780. *Memoirs of the Life of David Garrick, Esq.: Interspersed with Characters and Anecdotes of His Theatrical Contemporaries.* London: T. Davies.

Davies, T., 1784. *Dramatic Miscellanies.* London: T. Davies.

Downes, J., 1708. *Roscius Anglicanus, or An Historical Review of the Stage . . . from 1660 to 1706.* London: s.n.

Dunlap, W., 1833. *The History of the American Theatre.* London: R. Bentley.

Engel, L., ed., 2011. Sarah Siddons's Diva Celebrity. In: *Fashioning Celebrity.* Columbus: Ohio University Press, pp. 26–58 .

Engel, L., 2016. Stage Beauties: Actresses and Celebrity Culture in the Long Eighteenth Century. *Literature Compass,* 13(12), pp. 749–61.

Foot, J., 1811. *The Life of Arthur Murphy, Esq.* London: J. Faulder.

Friedman-Romell, B. H., 1995. Breaking the Code: Towards a Reception Theory of Theatrical Cross-Dressing in Eighteenth-Century London. *Theatre Journal*, 47(4), pp. 459–79.

Genest, J., 1832. *Some Account of the English Stage from the Restoration in 1660 to 1830*. Bath: H. E. Carrington.

Gilbert Austin, R., 1806. *Chironomia; or, a Treatise on Rhetorical Delivery*. London: T. Cadell.

Gollapudi, A., 2012. Selling Celebrity: Actors' Portraits in Bell's Shakespeare. *Eighteenth Century Life*, 36(1), pp. 54–81.

Halsband, R., 1983. Stage Drama as a Source for Pictorial and Plastic Arts. In: S. S. Kenny, ed., *British Theatre and Other Arts, 1660–1800*. London: Associated University Presses, pp. 149–70.

Hernandez, A., 2019. *The Making of British Bourgeois Tragedy: Modernity and the Art of Ordinary Suffering*. Oxford: Oxford University Press.

Highfill, P. H. J., Burnim, K. A. & Langhans, E. A. eds., 1973–93. *Biographical Dictionary of Actors, Actresses, Musicians, Dancers, Managers & Other Stage Personnel in London, 1660–1800*. Carbondale: Southern Illinois University Press.

Inchbald, E., ed., 1806. Remarks on The Fair Penitent. In: *The Fair Penitent*. London: Longman, pp. 3–6.

Johnson, S., 1817. Life of Rowe. In: R. Cumberland, ed., *British Drama*. London: C. Cooke, pp. v–xi.

Jones, R., 2013. Competition and Community: Mary Tickell and the Management of Sheridan's Drury Lane. *Theatre Survey*, 54(2), pp. 187–206.

Mayes, I., 1981. John Bell, The British Theatre, and Samuel de Wilde. *Apollo*, 113, pp. 100–3.

McGirr, E., 2014. 'Inimitable Sensibility': Susannah Cibber's Performance of Maternity. In: L. Engel & E. McGirr, eds., *Stage Mothers: Women, Work, and the Theater, 1660–1830*. Lewisburg: Bucknell University Press, pp. 63–79.

McGirr, E., 2016a. Authorial Performances: Actress, Author, Critic. In: J. Batchelor & G. Dow, eds., *Women's Writing, 1660–1830: Feminisms and Futures*. London: Palgrave, pp. 97–116.

McGirr, E., 2016b. *Partial Histories*. London: Palgrave.

McGirr, E., 2018. New Lines: Mary Ann Yates, The Orphan of China, and the New She-tragedy. *ABO: Interactive Journal for Women in the Arts, 1640–1830*, 8(2), p. Article 1.

Murtin, M. G., 2004. Robert Wilks. *Oxford Dictionary of National Biography*.

Neville, S., 1950. *The Diary of Sylas Neville 1767–1788*. Oxford: Oxford University Press.

Noggle, J., 2020. *Unfelt: The Language of Affect in the British Enlightenment.* Ithaca: Cornell University Press.

Nussbaum, F., 2010. *Rival Queens: Actresses: Performance and the Eighteenth-Century British Theatre.* Philadelphia: University of Pennsylvania Press.

Pascoe, J., 2013. *Sarah Siddons Audio Files: Romanticism and the Lost Voice.* Ann Arbor: University of Michigan Press.

Potter, J., ed., 1772. *Theatrical Review: or, New Companion to the Play House ... Calculated for the Entertainment and Instruction of Every Lover of Theatrical Amusements.* London: S. Crowder.

Ritchie, L., 2012. The Spouters' Revenge: Apprentice Actors and the Imitation of London's Theatrical Celebrities. *Eighteenth Century*, 53(1), pp. 41–71.

Roach, J., 1806. *John Brunton as Altamont and Miss Smith as Calista in "The Fair Penitent"*, London: J. Roach.

Roach, J., 1996. *Cities of the Dead: Circum-Atlantic Performance.* New York: Columbia University Press.

Roach, J., 2007. *It.* Ann Arbor: University of Michigan Press.

Rowe, N., 1703. *The Fair Penitent; a Tragedy.* 1st ed. London: Tonson.

Rowe, N., 1763. *The Fair Penitent.* BL11772a.5 ed. London: Tonson.

Rowe, N., 1768. *The Fair Penitent. A Tragedy.* Edinburgh: Martin & Wotherspoon.

Rowe, N., 1777. *The Fair Penitent, A tragedy. As It Is Acted at the Theatres-Royal in Drury-Lane and Covent-Garden London.* London: J. Wenman.

Rowe, N., 1806. *The Fair Penitent: A Tragedy in Five Acts . . .. with Remarks by Mrs Inchbald.* London: Longman.

Rubery, A., 2021. 'Thus Let Me Wipe Dishonour from My Name': Peg Woffington as Lothario in the Fair Penitent. *Theatre Notebook*, 75(2), pp. 76–93.

Russell, C., 2004. Merry, Robert (1755–1798), Poet. *Oxford Dictionary of National Biography.*

Shevelow, K., 2005. *Charlotte.* New York: Henry Holt.

Stern, T., 2012. Shakespeare in Drama. In: F. Ritchie & P. & Sabor, eds., *Shakespeare in the Eighteenth Century.* Cambridge: Cambridge University Press, pp. 141–60.

West, S., 1991. *The Image of the Actor: Verbal and Visual Representation in the Age of Garrick and Kemble.* London: St Martins.

West, S., 2004. *Portraiture.* Oxford: Oxford University Press.

Whalley, T. S., 1863. *Thomas Whalley's Journals and Correspondence.* London: R. Bentley.

Wilkes, T., 1759. *General View of the Stage.* Dublin: J. Coote.

Wilkinson, T., 1790. *Memoirs of His Own Life.* York: G. G. J. and J. Robinson.

Wilson, B., 2012. *A Race of Female Patriots: Women and Public Spirit on the British Stage, 1688–1745.* Lewisburg: Bucknell University Press.

Acknowledgements

The preliminary work for this Element was undertaken in a series of classrooms and rehearsal rooms with third year students on my Age of the Actress course at the University of Bristol. I am deeply indebted to and grateful for their insights into the openness of *The Fair Penitent* as a live text and their enthusiastic research into the lives and reputations of the actresses who embodied Calista

I would also like to thank my friends and colleagues who read drafts at varying levels of draftiness, especially Nush Powell, Katja Krebs, Freya Gowrley, Brett Wilson and Laura Engel. My thinking about eighteenth-century repertory and performance owes much to Misty Gale Anderson, Lisa Freeman, Nikki Hunt, Nora Nachumi, Chelsea Philips, Joseph Roach, Eleanor Rycroft, Stuart Sherman, Kristina Straub, David Francis Taylor and too many others to name here, but I am grateful to them all.

I gratefully acknowledge the support of the British Library and the University of Illinois, who provided access to physical and digital traces of past performances, including the actor's portraits and BL11772a.5, the heavily annotated *Fair Penitent* that models a way of engaging with playtexts.

Special thanks for Eve Tavor Bannet, who first convinced me to develop this Element and was a wonderful, supportive and insightful editor throughout the process.

Finally, I'd like to thank my family, from my husband, whose Hilton points and child-care enabled trips to archives and libraries, to my children, Clara and Alice, who left me alone long enough to finish writing.

I dedicate this Element to my students, past and future.

Cambridge Elements ☰

Eighteenth-Century Connections

Series Editors
Eve Tavor Bannet
University of Oklahoma

Eve Tavor Bannet is George Lynn Cross Professor Emeritus, University of Oklahoma and editor of *Studies in Eighteenth-Century Culture*. Her monographs include *Empire of Letters: Letter Manuals and Transatlantic Correspondence 1688–1820* (Cambridge, 2005), *Transatlantic Stories and the History of Reading, 1720–1820* (Cambridge, 2011), and *Eighteenth-Century Manners of Reading: Print Culture and Popular Instruction in the Anglophone Atlantic World* (Cambridge, 2017). She is editor of *British and American Letter Manuals 1680–1810* (Pickering & Chatto, 2008), *Emma Corbett* (Broadview, 2011) and, with Susan Manning, *Transatlantic Literary Studies* (Cambridge, 2012).

Markman Ellis
Queen Mary University of London

Markman Ellis is Professor of Eighteenth-Century Studies at Queen Mary University of London. He is the author of *The Politics of Sensibility: Race, Gender and Commerce in the Sentimental Novel* (1996), *The History of Gothic Fiction* (2000), *The Coffee-House: a Cultural History* (2004), and *Empire of Tea* (co-authored, 2015). He edited *Eighteenth-Century Coffee-House Culture* (4 vols, 2006) and *Tea and the Tea-Table in Eighteenth-Century England* (4 vols 2010), and co-editor of *Discourses of Slavery and Abolition* (2004) and *Prostitution and Eighteenth-Century Culture: Sex, Commerce and Morality* (2012).

Advisory Board
Linda Bree, *Independent*
Claire Connolly, *University College Cork*
Gillian Dow, *University of Southampton*
James Harris, *University of St Andrews*
Thomas Keymer, *University of Toronto*
Jon Mee, *University of York*
Carla Mulford, *Penn State University*
Nicola Parsons, *University of Sydney*
Manushag Powell, *Purdue University*
Robbie Richardson, *University of Kent*
Shef Rogers, *University of Otago*
Eleanor Shevlin, *West Chester University*
David Taylor, *Oxford University*
Chloe Wigston Smith, *University of York*
Roxann Wheeler, *Ohio State University*
Eugenia Zuroski, *MacMaster University*

About the Series
Exploring connections between verbal and visual texts and the people, networks, cultures and places that engendered and enjoyed them during the long Eighteenth Century, this innovative series also examines the period's uses of oral, written and visual media, and experiments with the digital platform to facilitate communication of original scholarship with both colleagues and students.

Cambridge Elements ≡

Eighteenth-Century Connections

Elements in the Series

A full series listing is available at: www.cambridge.org/EECC

Printed in the United States
by Baker & Taylor Publisher Services